Jump

from Suicidal Depression

to Skydiving

and Reality's Edge

Zoe Dolan

Cover image captured by: Rene Diaz. Used with permission.

for

my skybrothers

— especially Christian and Kenny

To Pamela —
with appreciation —

Zoe

"The pleasure of all things increases by the same danger that should deter it."

— Seneca

Prologue

I stood there, on the edge, leaning over.

The rust-colored mountains, into the tall rock faces of which the ancient city of Petra is carved, rose from the Jordanian desert, massive spurts of earth-blood that once gushed from our planet's core, then solidified.

This unimaginable other world's network of gorges streaked through time and space in the vastness below, and, atop the vantage point where I found myself, having hiked up from the sandy basin floor to a ridge so high it felt like the sky, red sandstone swirled out into an almost Martian landscape of dreams – as if cosmic fingernails had ripped apart earth's surface, and left chasms as scars.

I was nearing the end of a six-week trip. I'd landed in Athens, then ventured around the Aegean Sea and down to Crete before heading over to Rhodes and up to Istanbul and through central Turkey into Syria. After which I detoured over to Beirut – the late 1990s, remember, were back when Syria remained accessible and Lebanon had just become so – and subsequently, gasp, finally, made my way down here to southern Jordan, that is, in one last mini-sojourn before Tel

Aviv, where I'd catch my breath and a flight home.

I felt exhausted, and alone.

At age 23, nothing seemed to be working quite right. I couldn't manage a decent relationship, I was completely fucked up anyway, and this goddamn depression – which had been clouding over me for a decade now, ever since I'd started developing as a human being both intellectually and emotionally, since right before puberty, really – wouldn't lift.

You know.

We've heard it all before.

In my own case, however, I knew – with a conviction that has proven correct over the course of the last two decades – that the sadness never would go away, that this cloud would always remain.

Sure, there would be rays of sunshine from time to time, often whole days or even months or years of light.

But, the darkness would always be there, waiting.

And, one day, it would drift back overhead.

And gather strength and darken further.

And become too much.

So, I might as well just keep leaning.

And leaning.

And leaning.

Until I fell over.

Into nothingness.

And, you know what, I would have.

Except that, at the very instant, the instant of eternity right before I almost slipped away forever – a gust came blasting up the canyon wall.

The force held me there, suspended, for a second, before I stepped back.

Boy Meets Girl

Of course, I remain skeptical and everything, but oh shit is he cute. Also, he's smart in a farm boy-sexy way – and a carpenter... with those hands. OMG – those hands.

Did I mention he's two days younger than I? We're about to turn 40 in like six months.

We go out a bunch. He kisses me in the backyard under the lemon tree, beneath whatever stars the Los Angeles sky can muster.

Eventually I tell him I used to be a boy, too.

He's really nice about it – nicer than almost any of them has been before – but, in the end, it's the end.

We become friends, do things together, talk. We're very close. I depend on him. His voice always soothes me.

Months pass.

Somehow both of us end up tumbling into cryptocurrency around the same time – April of 2017 – right when shit's really popping off.

But then, unexpectedly, at the first Ethereal Summit – an overly intense blockchain slash community slash money slash art slash tech thing – I break down inside and ache.

I call him to say we can't interact anymore.

Neither of us needs any explanation that it's because I'm still in love with him. More so than ever.

Fuck.

Every time is the same, I think, walking to the subway in Brooklyn.

Every time but this time.

This time, somehow, is different.

I dissolve into a puddle of tears.

I cry so hard, and for so long, that my brain feels like it's spinning into the ground, and hurts.

The crying goes on for days.

I start making plans.

*

I experienced my first – and, so far, thank God, only – hospitalization when I was 18.

The medication made me fall over in the snow on the sidewalk and I didn't want to bother with getting my blood levels tested and all the rest. So I threw it out and white-knuckled myself afloat once more.

Darkness – that cloud – has hovered since, whether directly above or on the horizon, all the same, it's up there, threatening to come back anytime, as erratic and impulsive as mountain weather.

You understand. I know you do.

As expected, many days, many months are indeed better than others – yet, I have noticed that the dips, over the years, have grown deeper, the longer I've spent alone.

Like those valleys in Petra, the floors of which come closer and grow further away, simultaneously, through a parallax that tricks the mind.

And, my God, the years, the years! So many revolutions around the sun – so many, many years.

Man, more years have passed since those white knuckles than I ever expected to live. And I'm "only" in my early 40s – probably older by the time you read this.

I know life is precious. It's just I lost sight of how and have only begun to find out again.

*

You see, I'd never made plans before.

I'd thought about it, sure, but those previous attempts – perhaps "accident that I kept encouraging to go awry until I ended up in the hospital" and "other accident on the edge of a cliff, where the wind blew" would be a better way to put it – well, they were on a whim.

Now was different.

How can I make this one look inadvertent, so my mom won't be devastated? How can I arrange my affairs to leave everything clean and clear for my brother and his wife and their girls? How will I make sure it works, and I die? How can I – for fucking once on this earth – do something right?

And yet, I also wonder: Is this all there would ever be?

Is there really no other way?

I mean, instead of giving up, what if I were to give it one more year?

Just one year – one year – and see what happens then.

You know. I know you do.

One Year

"Life can be much broader once you discover one simple fact, and that is: Everything around you that you call life was made up by people that were no smarter than you."

– Steve Jobs

Month One: *The Change*

One day, about two weeks in, I would have missed waking up rested for the first time in a long while.

The nights that sleep has restored me have been few and far between, recently – I just cannot shake the worry that I am missing something while asleep – but, that problem appears to be resolving. I am starting to dream again – both in conscious life and subconsciously, I think. It has become increasingly difficult to tell a difference. Nor do I really wish to anymore; I would prefer an existence that melds the two.

We'll make our way to the dreams, eventually. I swear it to you.

*

That guy can't possibly be the Sun-bleached Blond Canadian Pilot – he's too old. The Sun-bleached Blond Canadian Pilot isn't so old yet.

Is he?

He must've sensed me peering in because he looked up from the bike he was tinkering with, suspended at chest level on a mount. When our eyes made contact, he motioned for me to come inside – perhaps he thought I was a customer or something – but I just smiled and shook my head, ever so slightly, and clicked my cycling shoes into the pedals and rode away.

Was that he?

It couldn't be.

Was it?

I rode a few blocks downhill to a little bench overlooking the Hudson River. I'd sat here so many times before, listening to music from the past and crying about lost time.

And thus I submerged into memories – many of which I've written about elsewhere – and drifted away: You know, just as the Sun-bleached Blond Canadian Pilot and I did together that one afternoon yesteryear we spent on his boat, you remember, when I swam topless and borrowed his t-shirt and almost mistook everything for normal.

At which point my phone signaled a text.

Wouldn't you know it, he *was* in the bike shop just now. The guy I'd seen and the picture in my mind of him collapsed into a bunch of years, and then expanded outward until they blew apart and singed the edges where I wanted the world to meet reality, like canyons in the sky.

Oh my.

Would he still seem sexy up close?

Less than five minutes later, I perched on a stool near the cash register, watching him finish up whatever he was doing – wrapping new grip around the handlebars or something – and trying to generate stuff to talk about, while endeavoring to relax into the flow, I guess, because, you know, what the hell, who cares.

The bike shop owner – a tall and thin gentleman ambling toward his twilight – dipped into our conversation here and there, providing a respite in the lulls.

Outside, the sky had darkened, and it had begun to sprinkle.

Side-story: Once upon a time, there was a Persian Cutie I crushed out on at the weekly spiritual gathering I used to go to in the West Village. I recall very little about him except that I wanted him to touch me all over and, one summer night, when I was wearing a polka dotted dress and heels, he exclaimed that riding my bike home in the rain would be fun!

Back to the moment: holy fuck. A dash across Manhattan is one thing. But...

The ride all the way back to New York City – at least until I can catch the subway on the other side of the George Washington Bridge – is going to suck ass...

And, did the temperature drop?

Maybe an Uber would be better...

Damn. The Sun-bleached Blond Canadian Pilot didn't bite. He wasn't going to offer a ride, apparently. And I wasn't going to ask, not outright.

It really was going to suck ass, riding twenty miles in the chilly downpour.

Le sigh.

At which point the bike shop owner volunteered a suggestion.

I cocked my head at him.

You think I should cycle twenty miles wearing a garbage bag?

Just watch. Everyone else on the road will wish they had one.

As he cut holes for my head and arms in this soon-to-be cycling poncho, I remembered something else he'd recommended years and years and years ago, when I had stopped by for a spare inner tube on a cold day: stuffing newspaper under my jersey.

Newspaper works great as a windbreaker — haven't you ever wondered why homeless people sleep all wrapped up in it?

My mind was already elsewhere as the Sun-bleached Blond

Canadian Pilot bent down to hug me goodbye.

I just love when they bend down and scoop me up like that.

Just love it.

Zoe! Pay attention.

Okay, I'd get some of the free local papers from the bakery just down the street – that's what I'd do. Perfect.

Yeah, okay, I'd be ridiculous covered in newspaper and a black garbage bag, speeding through New Jersey back to New York City, in the rain.

But, I'd be dry and warm…

And, suddenly, there it was: Oh shit, of all these rides home from Nyack over the last decade – there must be many many many dozens, probably a couple hundred by now – this one I'll fucking *remember*.

*

Yeah so the thing about the first month was doing things just because.

A ride through the rain – and, more so, the enjoyment of it.

A jaunt up to the Metropolitan Museum of Art. (And, along the way, a detour into some church I'd passed a thousand times but had never entered: a portal, it turned out, where pews

17

marched solemnly over checkerboard flooring toward the alter, which reared upward into a dome tiled in gold, lights shining overhead and filling the air with resplendence, like feelings in a room of a house I'd inhabited for decades, albeit removed as if by wormhole to Elsewhere.)

A schlep up to the roof of my apartment in the East Village to gaze at moonlight shining metallically through silvery clouds. (Would the whiteness of the moon have glistened any more brightly, if I had been with someone? Would I have seen the tremors of God's hands any less violently? Lie to me, it's okay, I promise.)

A return to that weekly spiritual gathering over in the West Village I told you about. (Sadly, the Persian Cutie remained long faded into the past without a trace, but, happily, I did get to see another man: the Mysterious Afghani, whose obsidian eyes all but shattered me to pieces. Oh, hells yeah! He had recently divorced and the energy that had always welled up between us could finally brim.)

You know, those types of *just because* lifedreams – the ones that leave us feeling like we just averted a car accident.

Month Two: *Noticing*

There was one Sunday evening, back in 2005, you may recall, just after I had returned to New York via Egypt (where I'd been living) from Thailand (where I'd had sex change surgery), and I dove into a swimming pool, in the right body, for the first time.

It was water polo practice, and, even though the dead of January raged outside, cold as a helluva bitch, here, inside the great big heated indoors swimming pool arena, the water enveloped me cool and refreshing, cascading over every square millimeter of my skin, washing away any trace of shame forever.

"I saw the angel in the marble and carved until I set him free."

That hokey quote attributed to Michelangelo sure is something.

Isn't it?

Anyway, where I'm going with this is that, one day during the second month, there I was, over a dozen years after that frigid winter day in New York, at water polo practice once again, only this time on a pleasant early summer morning out at the pool in Sherman Oaks, near Los Angeles, signing the ball that a stereotypically sexy Italian had purchased as a wedding present for our team captain and his fiancé, and I was like, I love that we get to live in an era when the stereotypically sexy Italian organizes this gift for his gay teammates.

Would I have noticed before? Probably.

But, would I have noticed myself noticing?

And noticed, also, how much the act of noticing infused the entire fucking world with hope, exploding into brightness that lasered outward to the end of time with beauty's vigor, as the angels of all our interactions (yours and mine and everyone else's) danced on tiptoes within and atop light beams, laughing, buoyant, gleaming joyful fury, hand in hand and wing against wing, tumbling together, just like we will in *The Sky and I*, which is coming.

It's coming.

Like the dreams.

I promise.

*

Just not yet.

Right so the thing about the second month was how the noticing began to change things.

It would still be some time yet – not long, but, even so – before I could see how I myself was changing, how the act of writing, every morning, "I would have missed..." – followed by the experiences that make life more than worth living, that render what might otherwise be unbearable into something not only bearable but perhaps wonderful somehow, or, on occasion, beyond transcendent –

How the mere act of writing was *engaging* me, in life, as I had never been before, anchored to magic in the world.

*

A guy in the airplane who reminded me to grab the hoodie that had been so, so hard to find, which had required a drive out to Pasadena and then further along the 210 to I don't even know where, like Monrovia or something.

A taxi driver only a few minutes afterward, whose sweetness of tone caressed the air like a million chameleons, soft as satin, surrounding me.

A trip for work out to jail in Buttfuck, New Jersey – past the sewage treatment plant which became all I could think about for several minutes, my God, the stench – because I've spent my adult life wondering where the seeker who I started out as went to, and where to find her, and now, in the bowels of nowhere, here was an adventure popping up, just like new experiences did when I was young and fresh to the world.

A warm afternoon punctuated by a guy probably half my age

checking out my legs whilst I sat reading in Washington Square Park. Mmm…

And, surprisingly, another afternoon spent in front of the computer. Because, after all, the pleasure of work can be a savior, as Mom often likes to remind me: Of everything else you *could* be doing right now, is there *really* anything you'd rather it be?

*

There was also a day when I would have missed Crystal Cove – a seaside California state park secreted along the coast north of Laguna Beach – giving me a tree bath in the basin of the canyon I always run down, and back up again, whenever I'm visiting Mom, that is, unless rain closes the trails and breaks my heart.

For, if I had not been there that particular morning, I would have missed the sounds of crackling branches and bird chirps and leaves rustling in the breeze, as I wondered what the crypto markets were doing and then let go.

And then the drive through town to Thousand Steps Beach, and the sand relinquishing to the ridges of my feet and bulging between my toes, and the invigoration that comes from walking into the ocean and body surfing and curling up like a potato bug within a wave – yeah I kind of knew where I was but also I lost track.

And the men and their chests and arms and faces and legs and feet – creatures that walk the earth for what amounts to the blink of an eye, before disappearing forever.

And, much later, the thought – amidst a conversation over dinner with Mom later that day – how a human being can be an accident. The entirety of a human life – perhaps any human life, for that matter – an accident that expulses a living being.

Maybe we are all accidents.

Month Three: *Daring for More*

One morning, I would have missed overhearing some random guy, as I jogged past him on my daily run, say, with a buoyancy in his voice, to whomever he was with, "How would everything need to be if you wanted to look back and say those were the best three years of my life?"

*

A few years ago, in 2013, I emailed Elyn Saks, a professor at USC Law School, to thank her for sharing her personal struggle living with schizophrenia, and some findings from a study of high-functioning people born with the condition, in a piece she wrote for the New York *Times*: "'Every person has a unique gift or unique self to bring to the world,' said one of our study's participants. She expressed the reality that those of us who have schizophrenia and other mental illnesses want what everyone wants: in the words of Sigmund Freud, to work and to love."

What strikes me even harder with the passage of time is Elyn's observation – which harmonized the changes that this project had begun effectuating within me by the third month – that "the seeds of creative thinking may sometimes be found in mental illness, and people underestimate the power of the human brain to adapt and to create."

And, so, here we were, five years later, wouldn't you know it, when there came a day on which, if I had been dead, I would have missed meeting Elyn, and getting to thank her, in person.

She was giving a talk for a continuing legal education seminar at the Federal Defender's Office in Los Angeles. I attended, alone, surrounded by others who had chosen indigent criminal defense as a career for the same reasons: love of our Constitution and devotion to individual liberty.

She remembered my email.

*

How curious: Weeding away what I could do without and keeping suicide as an option rendered each day so terribly exquisite.

If we could explain life, would it be the same?

If we saw rainbows everywhere?

Later I would see one – a rainbow – somewhere that would change absolutely everything.

Back in month three, however, steeped in a quotidian assembly line of days, I probably would not have missed the loneliness that *Big Little Lies* ground into me, what with those various couples interacting and having sex like normal human beings and all that shit.

You see – I know you do – I had yet to learn about finding happiness vicariously from others, in their joy.

But, not gonna obfuscate, I would very much have missed watching a character in the show fantasize about shooting her rapist in the face when he tried to break into her house, and then go to sleep with a gun under her pillow – because that is what I secretly wish I could do to my assailant, so I might never have to fucking think about him again, ever.

*

There is so much I want to share with you. Including this: when Elyn Saks spoke about getting married in her late 40s – and just not understanding the phenomenon of dating, and feeling like an alien whenever she would see couples out in the world up until then, I would have missed these fantasies murmuring inside me.

I probably also would have missed the sudden impulse to sell my crypto before the inevitable market crash, but then saying, *Oh, fuck it*, because, if it all goes to shit, I can just blow my brains out when this project ends, so who cares.

And, thus, there I was: a slightly different person – somewhat more skeptical, cynical, calculating, defensive, less trusting, more aware, and sadder, for sure – but also somehow happier, and erstwhile lighter: I was now a little more independent and therefore less caring, and certainly hungrier for risk, greedier, yet far more satisfied with what I have, you understand, further inclined to value my life as it is today, while also daring for more.

*

A goodbye kiss from a Sexy Colombian whose skin felt like a dolphin's, only with stubble – followed by a goodbye hug from the Grasshopper Taco Guy – at the beach after water polo practice.

A tiny lizard on a pillow atop the Japanese futon where I sit and read over my morning coffee.

A mass of human bodies in the pool at my Dear Baby-faced Lawyer Friend's birthday party – and the physicality of them against me, all radiant and friendly and who gives a shit about what's happening anywhere else for a minute, we're together right here right now, touching each other, playing, floating, letting go, as suspended in abeyance as our cares, for a few minutes this summer afternoon, this sliver of life.

Month Four: *Nipples, Dicks and the Start*

It was, come to think of it, a month of men.

The Persian who complimented my nipples at the Russian & Turkish Baths in the East Village, where I had started going topless because, you know, why not.

The guy who slowed his car as I cycled into Piermont, ten miles north of Manhattan, on my way to Nyack again, wearing a sports bra in the summer heat, to roll down the passenger side window and say: "Nice back."

The young man who pedaled by on a tree-lined Lower East Side street, watching from the corner of his eye. "Very pretty."

(Someone thought I was pretty?)

The dude at the Russian bathhouse in San Francisco, whose dick was totally getting hard as we chatted, naked, in the jacuzzi.

(It was a nice dick, really. Awesome, even.)

The runner out on one of the canyon trails in Crystal Cove, near the tree bath grove, who murmured, "Hey there, girl," and three others, the following day, who either said something or smiled, in almost the same spot.

And the LA-style type who came up to me at the Indian vegetarian on Sunset (a restaurant the Carpenter and I frequented adoringly until it abruptly closed) to apologize for looking at me this whole time. He thought he recognized me, he explained – and I kinda wasn't sure if he wanted me to forgive him?

They all surprised me but yo the one at the Indian vegetarian especially. Because, when you have trained yourself to have such low self-esteem – mostly as a defense mechanism to squelch hope altogether, before it even commences luring you into hoping your past may not matter, this time could be different, etc., etc. – you do not even entertain the possibility that anyone might be noticing you.

Or, at least, I don't.

*

I was sitting right where I had been when the Persian stared at my nipples, sweating, and a writer for a big magazine and I were talking and he was like, *You once said this thing, you know how there are some things you just remember or whatever, and I remember this one, wait, I wanna get it just right, yeah, okay: "In New York I miss the love, but in Los Angeles I miss getting fucked."*

Wow. You just never know when someone is listening, really listening, even a stranger, and you say something offhand that, for whatever reason, might stick for years, maybe for life.

You just never know.

Or, at least, I don't.

*

I would not have missed the thirty minutes I fretted over my crypto holdings before bed one night – suddenly, unexpectedly convinced that I had to sell it all immediately – but I would have missed the *Oh fuck it* part that follows whenever I remember that, at the end of this one-year endeavor, if it indeed everything goes to hell, I'm outta here.

*

And yet.

If I were dead, I would miss change. I would miss the dreams that wash over me when I consider possibilities. I would miss the lightness and forwardness and electricity of that process. And I would miss not only those things but also a secret I discovered I could have. I kinda didn't know I could have secrets before. That is, until there was a moment, in the fourth month, when I said to myself, *I need not tell this to anyone, and, indubitably, it will be better that way.*

*

One night, over dinner with the Healer after the Russian &

Turkish Baths, I would have missed her observe: *We think we are human beings trying to have a spiritual experience, when in fact we are spiritual beings trying to have a human experience.*

And then she complimented my life and thereby helped me gain perspective on the incalculable scope of what I may be grateful for.

In this fashion, I would have missed catching how, whereas in the *past* I'd have said I did not understand what she was saying – or should I say seeing, in me, since I usually feel like a failure, a nothing burger of a person, a waste – what I *now* said, instead, was that I did not understand because I see myself as normal.

Normal?

You mean, not some depraved vacuum of a non-entity, but a human being, like anyone else?

It was in that moment I began discovering how profoundly this project was changing me – for it was not just how I *chose* to react that had altered – but, indeed, *the underlying reactions themselves: my very instincts.*

You know: how they relate us to – and within – the world.

*

Earlier that day, the New York *Times* had featured a story about the 13th Street Repertory Theater – where I started

31

volunteering as a stagehand in my first theater job as a teenager – and the company's 100-year-old denizen Edith O'Hara.

I smiled at memories of her for several moments before time rolled on...

All the way into the following morning... when I would have missed a loving note from my former boss at the theater company where I went to work after 13th Street, in response to mine.

Turns out he and his husband had just been talking about me, and, look! Here I was, writing to him, out of the blue, about the *Times* feature.

You just never know when you've been remembered, or when people happen to be remembering you.

Or, at least, I don't.

But I was starting to.

Month Five: *Mindsculpting*

Everything from a guy kneeling on the sidewalk to tie his girlfriend's shoe – *What might it feel like to be she?* – to images, from the European Space Agency, of stars being born in our galaxy – *stars being born?!* – to a ride out to the end of the pier from which Piermont gets its name – *a derivation I never knew or stopped to consider before, would you believe it, a pier, of course, duh, Jesus, where the hell was I on all these bike rides through this little town, so many dozens and dozens of rides, probably hundreds, over the years.*

The years!

*

One night, in the subway – which I insisted on taking because there was no need for a cab, even though it was almost midnight – I would have missed a man who appeared to have almost no neck performing cello in the Times Square station. He breathed through a tracheal prosthesis, and his eyes, nose and mouth, compressed into about half the normal ratio, were situated down, relatively close to his chin. He was playing Elgar – quite lovingly – and his fingers graced the strings with aplomb. I would have missed contributing a larger donation than I usually do when subway musicians touch my heart, before vanishing down the stairs.

*

Two days later, if I had not taken the subway and then posted about the cellist, a successful crypto friend – whose event I attended at the same members-only club where I once met up with a British dandy grifter, who had like ulcers on his calves or something, it was weird – would not have mentioned how the experience impacted him.

If the successful crypto friend had not mentioned this impact, I would not have shared the story with the cute doctor he was talking with.

If I had not shared the story with the cute doctor, I would have missed the opportunity to connect with his humanity.

If we had not connected, I might have felt compelled to linger at the event longer, and, if I had, I would have missed talking in the sauna with my successful crypto friend's business partner, who also happened to cut out a little early, so he too might hit the Russian & Turkish Baths before closing time.

And, finally, if we had not gotten into such a deep conversation, I would not have entered the ambient heat Russian Room precisely when I did... which means I then would have missed saying, to a guy who was sitting next to me, "I hope you don't mind, but I wanted to tell you that you have one of the nicest bodies I have ever seen."

I got a little off on his faint German accent and staring into those caramel bronzite eyes of his – man, this draw toward guys of Korean heritage is a real thing – as we talked about educational systems and career bifurcation and a-mortality and crypto, in between dousing ourselves with cold water so we could enjoy the hotness together a tad longer.

*

Several days later, en route to the spa in Ktown following a flight back to Los Angeles, I'd have missed a long phone call with Mom that made me feel much better, despite the length of it resulting in the decision to forego a massage – which I ended up getting afterward anyway from some guy at Whole Foods, who had a massage chair set up near the cash registers!

He was even more fortuitous than whichever masseuse I'd have ended up with back at the Ktown spa because they're all women and I needed a man's touch. I would have missed letting myself go and pretending that his fingers on my neck were those of a lover I knew and trusted and who would be there for me and hold me and never let me go, as I soared away into a sky where dreams are made, like I used to back when I'd speed down Highway 1 after visiting my best friend from childhood at UC Santa Cruz, pounding *Closer* by Nine Inch Nails at full volume until I hit 100 mph, at which instant everything shitty that I had ever gone through would dissipate – if only for a moment – in the sunlight.

The depression fallout was very bad after this emotional lift, quite shatteringly – with the fantasy of blowing my brains out overtaking me all in an instant – so, I especially would have missed how swiftly my mind turned back to this project, and what I may have to look forward to tomorrow, and the next day, and the next…

*

Was all this mindsculpting – training thought on growth like a Bonsai tree – really fucking working?

Life had lost weight.

Month Six: *Now*

In the sixth month, I would have missed writing an *Ode to Men*:

I was born as a boy so I never really understood women talking about harassment from men

Until one put me in a chokehold and threatened me with death if I didn't submit

He was prosecuted and pleaded guilty because I thought what if he tries to do it again

It's just that men are so much stronger physically, and that's always the undercurrent

Just as it was when a mentor offered me a quid pro quo as a baby lawyer – for my career

Except by then I was strong enough to say I intended to get what I wanted on my own

And so I did – with a lot of help from good and sincere men along the way

The hard part is that the very things I like most in them – the strength and vigor and assuredness

Are also what I fear more than anything, when unbounded

The balance is as delicate as the characteristics are the opposite

And I know that men struggle with this very contradiction, too

The truth is I've flirted a little or liked a little flirting when maybe I shouldn't have

It's doubly convoluted for me being transgender because of the validation thing going on

It's triply convoluted because I'm getting older and the desirability thing is also going on

It's quadruply convoluted because sometimes I misread or find I've been misread

It's quintuply convoluted because sometimes it's invited – from both ends – but it's unclear

It's sextuply convoluted because, well, we're human

But it's like there's this line and somehow you just know

In the same way I know every woman instinctually recognizes Harvey Weinstein's tone

On that blood-curdling recording

And the president's on his

You know people say they're surprised when it happens "in certain environments"

But an education and money and power hardly mean you respect others

Some of the kindest men I've known had none of those things

And sometimes I can't help but wonder if that's why

Maybe all this talking about such an age-old phenomenon will make

things a little better
  Or maybe it'll simply confirm what we already knew
  I want to love men again, I really really really do
                              *

The Carpenter and I sat at the Indian vegetarian on Sunset –
remember? the one I mentioned we used to go to? – talking
about stuff.

I'd long since abandoned whatever self-defeating point I was
trying to make by not talking to him. We'd reconnected and
become brother and sister – because, you know, there is just
something about his voice, the stubble on his face at the end of
the day, those carpenter hands of his, the way he dresses like
for a photo shoot, whenever we go out, no matter where – and
it's like why starve ourselves of friendship, pointlessly, if we
really needn't.

After we'd eaten, I showed him a list I'd made the year
before, in some fit of desperation or whatever, on a single piece
of paper, breaking everything the fuck down in two columns:
each problem in my life on the left, and, on the right, the best
corresponding solution I could think of.

Although the effort got shuffled into a notebook shortly
afterward, where it stayed forgotten until I stumbled upon it
almost by accident – or, perhaps, fate, earlier today – there was

no denying that, twelve months on, I had worked through each line almost to a T.

Come on, make love to me.

Softly, so subtly at first, make our mystery for us – do it gently – but, please, take control, and envelop and vanquish every uncertainty.

Just for a minute.

I really really really want it.

Now.

*

A praying mantis that lay dying on the steps to the backdoor, which I almost stepped on, as I ascended, on the way up after my morning run, and which I placed in a potted bougainvillea, where, you know, maybe it might feel more comfortable among nature. *This insect was – I see now – a portal to sympathetic fibrous strings of the universe, vibrating, spindling outward past our solar system, speeding up into other dimensional aspects of shared reality, tinged and tinted with the selflessness of kindness that I should aspire to, every minute.*

Two sentences from Elena Ferrante's *My Best Friend*: "She stopped to wait for me, and when I reached her she gave me her hand. This gesture changed everything between us forever." Many other Kindle readers had highlighted the same passage. *Who are the other human beings around the world, likewise identifying with these encapsulations of human experience, and how do I find them?*

One day when, more than anything else, as always, I would have missed accepting that my heart has broken beyond repair. *Like an overgrown forest, I must burn to the ground before I may grow again — but do so I may, now less encumbered.*

*

That artist in Grammercy, standing on the corner of Irving Place and 18th Street, painting with an easel as if we were in early 20th Century Paris or some shit, and not present-day Manhattan. I mean, he even wore a beret.

The National Arts Club, across from the park a few blocks north, where I caught exhibits by a Mexican artist and gender-bending self-portraitist girl-boy.

A crane lifting a giant piece of glass toward some high-end loft, suspended above the street.

This Middle Eastern restaurant named, um, Almayass. (Say it out loud, slowly.)

And then other things...

An exhibition-experience-marketing-ploy type thing called *Noah's Ark*, designed by Robert Wilson, where you ventured inside this giant box and the lights went out and you heard thunder and lightning and then windows, these tiny windows, lit up, featuring pairs of exquisite diamond-encrusted animals – earrings, broaches, pins – costing hundreds of thousands of dollars each.

A walk down the High Line – for the first time, like the pier in Piermont, after all these years, you see, now that I was *engaging*, I found myself on errant adventures I'd meant to embark upon all along, but instead kept saying I'd get to later, well, fuck it, later was now, I could be dead this time next year – where I took in the huge murals and surrounding apartments, with their walls of glass, almost voyeuristically.

A subway car pulsing with color inside – and a violinist electrifying the 14th Street A-C-E station with his fierce-ass rendition of Michael Jackson's *Billie Jean* – on my way to meet a friend after his cancer diagnosis.

And to think: All that – from the artist to the friend with cancer – was a single day.

One day.

Halfway through our year together.

Is this world even real?

Month Seven: *Purpose*

It was a war I'd been waging for a long time. I know I haven't told you yet, but, the same week that the Carpenter admitted we'd be a no go because of my past, our nation's largest federal district – the Central District of California, headquartered in Los Angeles – terminated me from a panel of defense lawyers representing poor folks, in retaliation for standing up to judicial interference with the administration of justice.

As a federal criminal defense lawyer, I wrote in my Medium exposé, *I get front row tickets to the imploding hot mess that is the United States of America. I've saved a seat for you.*

Then I just delved right the fuck into it.

It's more than just how rules of evidence and procedure are written to benefit the government and secure convictions. It's more than just how the system skews toward the prosecution over the defense – in everything from judicial interpretation of the Bail Reform Act (which was once intended to reform the bail process), to insurmountable jury instructions that end up swallowing human conduct like a black hole, to Draconian sentencing guidelines that lead to unnecessarily long sentences.

The problem is that many judges – the very people who are supposed to ensure that everything is played down the middle – demonstrate bias against defense advocacy.

I talked about how they – those power-wielding judges – control the purse strings of indigent defense, even though, when Congress initially promulgated the underlying legislation that handed over this power in the 1960s, it wasn't supposed to be that way long-term. Eventually, we were supposed to have a Defender General of the United States – just as we have an Attorney General of the United States (who oversees the federal prosecutorial function).

In modern day Los Angeles, by this point, things had gotten so shitty for indigent defense lawyers that the court's "panel" of qualified attorneys had declined by over one-third in just a few years.

Some, like me, were kicked off. Others had simply resigned.

Meanwhile, I – can you believe it – had the *temerity* to maintain my clients' challenges to the court's unconstitutional intrusion into defense management.

*

Being terminated for standing up on behalf of Americans' right to have an independent lawyer, pursuant to the Sixth Amendment provision for counsel, initially did not phase me. After all, I was doing my job – and, I knew, in my heart, I was following through on the oath I took to defend our Constitution when I first became a lawyer all those years ago.

But, I am human like anyone else, and the court's retaliation against my advocacy – coupled with another problem: withholding of compensation for months and months of work I'd performed on numerous cases, including a jury trial I won – eventually wore me down.

*

It was not until nine months later, when I dissolved into that puddle of tears over the Carpenter I was telling you about at the very beginning, that I realized the extent of what had happened: Both he and my profession had rejected me in the same week.

For these nine months – the gestation period for human life – I came to see how I'd been living with the message, both in work and love, that I was worth nothing.

Nothing.

*

Now, in sharing my story publicly, I had fought back. I had done the right thing for my clients, and I'd live having put forth every effort I could in hopes of helping make one little, typically ignored corner of our country better.

Consequences be damned – no one could hurt me anymore.

I was free.

A bird in the sky.

Flying.

*

The hottie in the Russian Room at the Baths who resembled an elf – but, like, a *Lord of the Rings* elf, you know, the tall and lithe kind – who talked to me of Wittgenstein, as we sat there on the wooden slabs laid across the stone benches, our nipples (remember: I go topless) facing one another.

These lines of poetry by Czeslaw Milosz: She gets up from her rumpled sheets. / In her dreams she thought of dresses and travel. / She walks up to the black mirror. Youth didn't last long.

And other such reminders that, no matter what is unfolding beyond our control, sometimes the tiniest things will keep us aloft.

Month Eight: *First Times*

We are not always as invisible as we might think, and, to me at least, there seems little in life more remarkable, and yet so organic to being human, than friendships that endure. What brings us together and holds us there?

You know, thoughts like that one, which I would've missed writing down.

*

New Year's so rarely seems like a fresh beginning, and, yet, this one did.

In the preceding days, I'd built my first computer, and, at a party the night before, I'd kissed a woman. So, now, this warm and sunny morning, I decided to go on a hike and take some pictures. Only thing is, I got around to it so late in the day that the vanishing sunlight prevented me from capturing, with my phone, the majesty I saw in Topanga Canyon – its splendor lies in the details – while simultaneously adjusting for such unwieldy mountain shadows.

Reality got lost in translation to permanence.

I mean, I could show you the sun reflecting on the Pacific

Ocean from the peak where I stood at the trail's end, but, because of how light works, I could not show you everywhere else — not all at once.

Or so I thought.

That is, until I turned around and the sun came out from behind the clouds and speckled this edge of the world with gold — an image my phone *did* capture — because perhaps we can, in fact, share a moment that we thought has escaped, if only we wait.

*

I went 'round and 'round that hairy portion of the 10 freeway — near where it breaks off down into the 5 and over into the 60 — exiting and then circling back through various neighborhoods to get on again — in search of a spot from which to contemplate some graffiti on an overhead sign, suspended there in space above the center lanes, I mean, how did the artist even get up there?

If I hadn't gotten lost on one of those circle backs, I'd have missed happening upon a gigantic graffiti mural covering an entire building wall, on some random block south of the 10, that literally exploded into a stalwart expression of orange-red tags and symbols which were, on further reflection, probably entities from another place, torso-sized imaginings that mirror the expression of existence, strutting across the low sky and pouncing out at passers-by like me, punching us with Los Angeles glamgrit.

At the center: a toddler on the shoulders of his father, or maybe his uncle, his fist around a can of spray paint aimed into the air.

A sudden galaxy of intricate design elements and cross-cultural modalities, a modern greyscale Orson Wells gangsta overlaid upon a massive mandala radiating outward in brain-squiggles, then emanating further into a startling, bright blue cartoon rodent being, alive with pellucid pale sea-green and deep magenta irises.

A cascade of faces and facial parties, mostly in blues.

Another rodent being – this one purple and crouched, its front bunny teeth exposed and dripping with blood, as a pistol emerged from the intertwisting of universal strings (or perhaps fibers of human confusion), converging above a hidden and forgotten parking lot (where, let's be honest, who knows what's happened over the years).

A cubist, thin man-creature with ever-so-slightly bulbous edges, levitating a top hat that wouldn't even fit his baby, accompanied by a mysterious witch with swelling lips and pretty button nose features and a toppling pyramid of forest hair, around the side of which a red-eyed goat — a scout from an Elsewhere who's gotten into the Waking, I imagine — stared at you.

What a detour.

Finally, I made it back to the 10 and snapped a photo of the tag overhead I'd been trying to get to this whole while.

*

Dolores O'Riordan's death culminated in this memory I shared on Twitter: *Sitting here listening to The Cranberries' "Put Me Down"— the song I played on repeat as I rode the bus through the Sinai Peninsula at dawn for the first time, aged just 19 years old, and the world was blue like a lunar landscape and my entire life lay ahead — and it's omg almost too much.*

Wouldn't you know it, A Dear Friend From College happened to see my tweet immediately, and, the next thing I knew, I would have missed her replying that she felt one of my replies with all her heart:

I do not want to be old, I do not like it at all

Even though I absolutely love being 40, which is weird

Whatever

Anyway everyone says I'm crazy but I would give anything to be 19 again

Fucking anything

I miss soft eyes with which to see the world

Mostly I miss first times

*

Now I can look back.

And see what I missed before: Building a computer, the kiss, sunset on New Year's in Topanga, the portal to Elsewhere south of the 10 – each of these instants, and so many more – were firsts.

Month Nine: *Love*

If I hadn't been here for the ninth month, I would have missed kneeling on my morning run through the park, and, as I ran my fingers through the dewy green, wondering why we call them blades of grass when they're so soft.

I also would have missed rock climbing outdoors for the first time: A friend from high school and her husband took me along to scale a 750-foot mountain face – that is, a seven-pitch (seven-stage), all-day climb in the Red Rock Canyon National Conservation Area outside Las Vegas. Afterward, as I slumped in a booth at the casino nearby, inhaling guacamole and chips as if they were the last food on earth, I wanted more than ever to be alive.

What I want to tell you is what you may already have guessed: I'd have done neither – touch the grass or rock climb a fucking mountain – but for this project.

*

Meanwhile, at 5Rhythms dance class – where it was so astonishing to be part of an experience that involved people ranging from their 6s and 7s to their 60s and 70s – I'd have missed the Olive-Skinned Instructor (who reminds me of every

Israeli I've ever crushed out on) playing a remix of *Dreams* by The Cranberries, which brought me to tears over how the last two decades flashed by.

I would have missed dancing through this compendium of savage beauty, as I allowed myself to slip out of the moment and ponder what I wanted to convey to Don't Fuck This Up – my new name for the woman I kissed on New Year's Eve.

Because I knew what would happen when I did – or, perhaps, as a grenade-throwing tactic – I preemptively opened myself up to someone new: another dancer, who sat on the bench across from me following class, as we tied our shoes, and whom I'd felt an attraction to for a few years now.

His name sounded like an Indian god's. He clasped my hand three times longer than normal, upon which I told him that he has beautiful skin.

This heavenly creature was pushing through fear and vulnerability right now, as well, just as I was, it turned out – and so our Goodbye stung all the more poignantly as I smiled in retreat to an unoccupied ballet training room, on the floor below, where, sitting on a chair amidst the emptiness, I wrote a love textstorm to Don't Fuck This Up.

I divulged a lot, including how the most compelling moment of kissing her was not so much when she lunged over the armrest to make out some more – after I had picked her back up from the airport to make-out, so we could devour each other while she awaited her delayed flight – although that was extraordinarily hot – but, rather, several moments later, when she touched my hand, for the first time.

What is it about this gesture that contains such multitudes?

She called a few hours later, like two hours following the textstorm, to pull the plug on everything.

*

I would have missed the tailspin that the collapse of our budding relationship sent me into precisely because, almost instantly thereafter, I began to rebound – mostly, I think, due to how this project had rearranged me and calibrated reactions to disappointment.

*

As I began to surface from the blackness, out of curiosity, I snuck back in time to a love e-mail I wrote to a guy when we were young, in that magical moment at the end of the millennium in New York:

Just before we met I stood in Times Square watching the snow swirl about in the lights. Despite the wind there was calmness in the air – or at least I felt the serenity within me and it was so strong it made the world seem tender. As soon as we saw each other I wanted to kiss you. A part of me says it was your eyes, another your smile, another just the moment itself. There were forces at work. Now, sitting on the carpeted stairs of the theater lobby, I feel them.

Perhaps the best way to express love at first sight is to experience it. A destination can be reached in many ways, and there are many journeys along each way. Or is there only one way, after all? We believe in choice until we suddenly have no choice — a situation which may be more beautiful than we ever imagined. Do you believe we can know something, ever? We might have a good argument over that because I don't. I barely believe that you are real, that you could continue to be real, and that the feelings I already have are not being tossed out into the void of fate and chance that gives us, every so often, our illusions.

I know that I want to share with you. Looking into your eyes gives me something I yearn for always: hope. The clarity of your expression... The height of your energy... Your soul is strong.

Writing these words almost scares me. But what really does scare me is the idea of missing an opportunity with you. I suppose it's best to move gradually, and with deliberation. But I want to be with you so much. When I close my eyes I can see your lips right before we kissed, in the subway station at 50th and Broadway, yesterday, the last time I saw you. I also see you bending over the server in the Com room, then looking up, smiling at me. I still feel myself standing next to you, gazing at the *moles on your beautiful, edible neck, bugging you to kiss me while you finished up your work. And I get [excited] thinking about how we could not stop kissing each other in the street, under the umbrella, nearly falling over each other into the snow.*

A couple of hours later, I tweeted:

yesterday I got creamed in love again

I compared

my last love textstorm to her

with a love e-mail to a guy from 19 years ago

wow

they could have been the same

all these years

I have loved

in the same way

seen love

the same

felt love

the same

love has remained unchanged

so have I

*

As you'll have guessed, were it not for this project, I probably wouldn't have risked my heart again.

Month Ten: *Everyday Wonder*

If I had ended my life before this project began, in the tenth month I would have missed:

How my hand shot out to catch a fall when I missed one of the back stairs outside. I was carrying stuff and managed to hang onto a bunch of it. The human body — however the hell it manages to interact with instinct and the brain — is a remarkable creation.

How I felt — as I drove to Thai after the spa in Ktown, and then again on my way up the hill back home — very much at home here in Los Angeles. It took four years, but, it happened: The sensation has imbued my bones. Here's a secret: I would miss being externally in the middle of something far greater than I alone could ever imagine — and yet pinpoint enough to apprehend with imagination.

How I like the dark edges of life. The bad angels. The taste of saliva that seems almost like someone else's. The origins of love. Independence. Grandeur. Brutality. The astonishing plain beauty of everyday wonder.

*

A passage about traveling in *Love, Africa: A Memoir of Romance,*

War, and Survival by Jeffrey Gettleman that struck me just so – and thereupon the reliving, within my mind's eye, of that moment in Cairo when I encountered a heartful young man who had come to Egypt for the first time, at the same tender age of 19, as I myself had done, when I expressed a sentiment to him that I've written about before: *"Travel," I said. "Take the overnight train down to Luxor and Aswan, take the bus to the Sinai and climb Mount Catherine for the sunrise, visit the desert oases and especially Siwa," I said, thinking of the Temple of Amun. "Do not wait for anyone else to go with you. Just go. Go everywhere and see everything you can. You will never regret it."*

*

Another 5Rhythms dance class – one where, at points, I felt like I was flying.

When it ended, I lay in the fetal position staring at the hand of a man next to me, his fingers, the veins running toward his wrists, his skin, sort of transfixed by beauty: We are born, by a series of accidents that have been happening since before Time's beginning, we somehow come into these bodies here on this earth, we eat this stuff called food and breathe this thing called air and go through this experience called life – and, somehow, the universe congeals, for the briefest flickers of its history, into this organism of protoplasm that walks and talks and thinks and feels and attracts other organisms of protoplasm and communicates with them and transfixes them, as I was: this guy's hand, for me, in that moment, embodied – emhanded – what it means to be human.

Whereupon, wouldn't you know it, the instructor – none had ended a class I'd attended this way before, not in all the years I'd been going – said, *Reach out and touch someone near you.*

Now, look – in another twist of exquisite unfolding – this instructor, back like four or five years prior, was the first person I danced *with* at 5Rhythms – I mean, the first person I ever even made physical contact with during a dance – you know, it was sort of like kissing, except with our foreheads and our arms: We were moving closer to and away from each other and then back together, in unison, and I could feel his breath and it was when a part of me awakened forever.

This same part, mind you, was the one that lay there in this moment a few revolutions around the sun later, burgeoning quietly with subtle reverie: Would you believe – here I was, suddenly, reaching out, touching, holding the very hand that had just held the whole universe for me.

OMG.

Hey there.

I so want us to touch.

Right here, in the Dreaming.

Together for an ever.

You and me.

OMG.

Month Eleven: *A High and Beautiful Wave*

On April Fools' Day, I would have missed looking back on how lucky I've been to find myself in the right place at the right time so very, very often, and wondering whether I might sink or fly with whatever unfurls next – as much as, if not more than, I'd've missed saying, *Well, here goes everything.*

*

Less than a week later, a dm arrived from a lawyer from Greece – he follows my Twitter and was just saying *Hi* – with the "wave speech" from Hunter S. Thompson's *Fear and Loathing in Las Vegas*:

There was madness in any direction, at any hour. If not across the Bay, then up the Golden Gate or down 101 to Los Altos or La Honda... You could strike sparks anywhere. There was a fantastic universal sense that whatever we were doing was right, that we were winning...

And that, I think was the handle – that sense of inevitable victory over the forces of Old and Evil. Not in any mean or military sense; we didn't need that. Our energy would simply prevail. There was no point in fighting – on our side or theirs. We had all the momentum; we were riding the crest of a high and beautiful wave…

*

What brings us together and holds us there?

Is it this fundamental commonality of human experience: this ineffable, ungraspable, and yet viscerally overwhelming sense of recognition, the energy that flows from an encounter with another human being – living or otherwise, before our very eyes or Elsewhere – who *understands*?

*

You might say that the noticing I wrote about in *Month Two* culminated in experiences like remembering to kneel, seven months later, in *Month Nine*, and touch the grass.

But, seriously, the real bee's knees materialized now, one random morning in *Month Eleven*, when I stopped to softgaze at them – softgaze at an actual bee's knees, I mean, those miniscule joints, replete with tiny bulbs of pollen – as hundreds of the insects buzzed around a huge flowering bush, atop this one mountaintop path on my daily run, overlooking the San Gabriel Mountains.

Have you ever noticed pollen on a bee's knees before? I never had.

And then, three days later – one day after the Hunter S.

Thompson dm, which happened in between — there was another moment on that mountaintop path. Except this time I softgazed further out, at the valley below, though not quite all the way to the mountains, and wondered what the very first human being to set foot up here might have thought.

Have you ever paused to consider what the first person to stand where you currently are might have been thinking, at that instant? I never had.

*

I emerged from the whirlpool at the club, tingling — that feeling alone is enough to stay alive and keep on keeping on for — and made my way into the quiet room and sank into a lounge chair, with a warm blanket wrapped around me. As I showered off before getting dressed, I thought, *My God, I don't need a big expensive house, I don't need to travel to five-star resorts in all corners of the world — I can just come here, to this little spot hidden away in downtown LA.*

By later that week, I didn't even need to drive anywhere anymore: The warm breeze of late afternoon on my skin, as I lay in my hammock between the lemon and apple trees out back — near where the Carpenter kissed me — was more than enough.

*

Fuck.

I'd been rampaging through this year, one day after another, without relent, thinking I'd never reach the end, which had heretofore loomed like a forever, past the reach of conception, some faraway dream I could taste the desire for but never touch.

And, yet, here it was – the eleventh month.

Time was nearly up.

So, I hiked all day to the Bridge to Nowhere, nestled deep in those San Gabriel Mountains, and, hooked and strapped to a bungee cord system, leaped off.

And then, like the following weekend or whatever, I headed out to a "dropzone" over in Perris Valley to the east, boarded an airplane, rode up to 12,500 feet, and, hooked and strapped to a Puerto Rican dude I'd met about twenty minutes before, leaped out.

Month Twelve: *Flying*

Of course my main parachute would open up to a line twist on my very first unattached skydive!

What I would have missed – though I didn't even realize it until after I'd landed – is how I went into dealing with that emergency in accordance with my training from the day before: by spinning myself around and pedaling my legs, and, then, once I was straightened out, going straight into a canopy control check.

It did not even occur to me that I had a potentially life-threatening problem – all alone – 5,000 above the ground.

All I knew, in those instants of eternity, was calm.

*

Another thing I would have missed about that jump – although, again, it didn't catch up with me, or, rather, *I* didn't catch up with *it*, until later – was the communion I experienced with my instructors and the Kind-eyed Cameraman during freefall.

Wow: Was that electric spiritual current a collective brain meld, as we plummeted at terminal velocity toward the earth, or what?

*

Soaring above the very world I had so longed to escape just one year before, on my virgin flight under solo canopy, I'd have missed becoming a new person – more humbled, yet less afraid – and, of course, sharing what happened next, with you.

The Sky and I

"Every time that I have gone up in an aeroplane and looking down have realized that I was free of the ground, I have had the consciousness of a great new discovery. I see I have thought this was the idea and now I understand everything."

– Isak Dinesen, *Out of Africa*

Jumps 1 and 2: *I Saw the World*

He was about my height and around my age, and scruffy. His eyes, dashing golden brown fields of hay swaying under gusts of molasses, shone with a twinkle. I don't remember whether he smiled, but I'm almost as sure as you are that he must have.

I mean, how else would an instructor introduce himself before a first tandem skydive.

What the fuck am I doing?

I liked that he was Puerto Rican. I had only visited the island once, several years before Hurricane Maria. The trip had been a treat from some Craigslist date who developed an instant crush on me and then, as time passed, became a friend whose authenticity always lifted my spirits – even mornings after he stayed up the whole night snorting cocaine.

I've felt closer to Puerto Ricans in general ever since the storm. Not that Hurricane Sandy left quite as much destruction in its wake – and yet, when I close my eyes, I can still see the sky light up white as an eggshell, when something in the powerplant seven blocks north of my old apartment in the East Village exploded, and water from the East River came creeping, and then suddenly flowing faster and faster, up the block toward our building, cascading over the well out front and filling up the basement – coming within inches of my home, closer and closer – before receding...

I stared into those alluring brown eyes, just as I had bored into those of my surgeon in Bangkok before sex change surgery – asking myself all that mattered in such a moment: Could I trust this human being, whom I knew nothing about, with my life?

Hurricane bonding aside.

My training, such as it was, had comprised one short video and a series of waivers – one after another stating, in various permutations, that I understood skydiving was an inherently dangerous activity and I could die and I and my heirs would therefore give up my right to pursue any remedy in the event of injury or death and no one would sue the dropzone or anyone affiliated with it for any reason ever.

You know. You've been through the drill.

Of course I could trust him.

It was his life up there, too, after all. Both of ours together.

*

The next thing I knew, I was farting with each step as we approached that great big door at the back of the sky van –

expelling whatever air my body conjured out of nervousness or perhaps terror: the same heart-quickening excitement, bubbling with shock, that had seized me and electrified my blood during our entire ride to altitude – an interminable fifteen minutes that had flashed by quicker than a year of life...

An eternity to the door, gone by in an instant –

Oh my God, we were outside now, in the motherfucking sky, flipping a gainer even though we weren't supposed to, I mean, that video from before only said I was supposed to arch, hips down toward earth, pointing at the world; this flip was an unexpected development, and the horror of it nearly sent me into paroxysms, apoplectic in this fraction of a second that lasted forever, that is, as we stabilized and then accelerated toward terminal velocity, whereupon the fear dissipated and everything I'd ever thought I'd known or experienced converged into one enlivening, all-encompassing surreality that overtook me and shredded every sensation into bliss.

Holy shit.

*

It's conceivable.

I mean, yeah, sure, you *might* be able to conduct some sort of exhaustive search, casting your net across the southern half of California or whatever, and, against the odds, find two hotter men.

But, I doubt it.

"Thank you in advance for saving my life," I said to the dirty blond one, my Accelerated Free Fall (AFF) Level One main instructor, as he checked my gear a second time.

"You're responsible for that," he admonished gently, looking up at me. "We're just your backup."

What was about to go down was still penetrating me. My decision to go through with a skydive wearing my own parachute had only started hitting yesterday, halfway through our first jump course, when the instructor had whipped out pictures of malfunctions.

I'm not sure what I'd assumed — that canopies just always opened properly?

"This part is meant to scare you," she said, seeing our faces.

And then, after a moment, holding up a placard with a clearly fucked up canopy, she queried: "What do you do if see something like this?"

"Emergency procedures," we all repeated, in a chorus.

"And what are they?"

"Look red, grab red, peel, pull. Look silver, grab silver, peel, pull. Arch."

"Show me."

We all gazed at where our red and silver emergency handles would be and started to demonstrate.

"Say it out loud as you do it," she reminded us.

"Look red, grab red, peel, pull. Look silver, grab silver, peel, pull. Arch."

"Again."

"Look red…"

I looked down, slightly embarrassed.

"You're right," I exhaled. "Of course."

How quickly it was all unfolding.

Wasn't it just a few minutes ago that they'd called my name and I'd headed to the gear-up area?

The seconds flew by, unrelenting.

Washing off my goggles with Windex and a stray paper towel.

Fitting a medium-sized helmet and tightening the strap.

Checking my altimeter to ensure it was set to zero.

Leaving the student gear-up area: my God, what next?

Walking past the boarding area. Less than ten minutes now.

In a mock-up, going through the dive flow, one last time.

Repeating each phase: arch, check-in, three practice touches on the small faux leather ball connected to the pilot chute that would catch air and extract my main canopy, altitude check every four-to-five seconds, lock on at 6,000, wave off and pull at 5,500 feet...

Going through it again...

Hyper-conscious that my voice, scurrying out of a throat dried by desert air and the sheer import of what was happening, sounds deep, like a guy's – but not caring because I have a parachute strapped on and I'm about to board an airplane, so who the fuck cares...

I mean, who the fuck –

My main instructor, noticing my tension, drifting into my consciousness to intervene: "Yeah... you're skydiving! Right around here, you start relaxing."

And then, pointing to the Kind-eyed Cameraman: "He's gonna be flying in front of you – smile and give him the thumbs up... Okay, 6,000..."

Wave off and pull at 5,500 feet...

*

Reserve instructor?

78

You mean I can lose the first one?

It was on the ride up, when he was seated next to me, that I noticed how his profile resembled the stark definitions of the first boy I ever slept with, twenty-five years ago.

A quarter century.

A lifetime in and of itself.

Several lifetimes, and many more over.

An eternity of an instant, that time.

2,500? That's my final decision altitude – whether I can fly my main canopy or need to cutaway.

He sure is hot.

5,500? That's pull time.

They both are.

The dive flow? Arch, check-in, three practice touches on the small faux leather ball connected to the pilot chute that'll catch air and extract my main canopy, altitude check every four-to-five seconds, lock on at 6,000, wave off and pull at 5,500 feet...

Yes.

Yes, I'm ready to skydive.

12,500 feet.

The door was open.

Everyone before us had left.

My God.

I later observed, in the video, how I clenched my main instructor's shirtsleeve all the way to the door…

and, as we stood there, at the edge, my heels hanging over into the sky, I gave the count…

ready… set…

pausing for an extra second – hesitating – for an instant of eternity – before the go…

and suddenly I hopped back and out.

My last thought was the same as on the table before sex change surgery:

I

saw

the world…

Both times everything went black.

*

Except, this time, the blackness only lasted the four breaths they had told me to take as I arched…

BREATHE.

ARCH.

BREATHE.

ARCH.

BREATHE…

Arching…

Breathing…

As the world came back into focus and a wave of splendor hit.

"You're skydiving!"

And, sure enough, there he was: the Kind-eyed Cameraman, in front of me, smiling widely.

Hey, you.

I smiled and stuck out my tongue and gave him a thumbs up with both hands – which otherwise clenched the air in anxiety, like a Gremlin's gnarled paws, holding all the emotion I couldn't feel yet and maybe never would…

"You're skydiving!"

Oh, fuck…

That went by fast.

It's pull time and where is that goddamn little ball, the one I'm supposed to pull to extract my pilot chute, which in turn should catch air and extract my main, that is, if everything were working as intended, which it was not, because I couldn't find that goddamn ball, at least until I felt my main instructor's hand on my Gremlin paw, gently placing my fingers arou–

PULL.

*

They hadn't told us anything about steering, really, at least not that I remembered.

Whatever. I was under a canopy above the earth.

It was...

the most

incredible

experience

of

my life.

*

"Oh, yyyyyyyyou're the one who stuck out her tongue."

"Yes," I murmured, taking the flash drive with the video she'd edited.

"You're one of us," she chuckled.

And then, a moment later, as she cast her eyes over the

counter and back up at me: "Welcome home."

Jumps 3 – 9: *The Journey*

My second unattached skydive.

I was neither accustomed to the proposition of jumping out of an airplane – I shook my head as I sat in my car in the parking lot: *What am I doing this for, exactly?* – nor why, let alone how, I was supposed to move myself and my instructor forward and "drag" him "across the sky."

He promised the experience would be fun for him – and my reserve instructor, as well.

Fabulous. Yeah.

I mean, I got the mechanics of what I was being tested on: whether I could extend my legs and pull my arms in toward my shoulders – kinda like pushing and clawing my body across a bed of air blasting at me from below, supposedly – but, srsly, WTF.

Also, this main instructor – who seemed to be avoiding eye contact – came off as vaguely weird. He was older than the others and it was a weekday – why wasn't he working?

Then again, why wasn't I?

His bright blue eyes caught the light like ice.

I've never trusted blue eyes.

We talked about criminal defense. If he had it to do all over again, he mused, perhaps that's what he'd have done.

At which point he did that thing where we sort of bunch our lips in on one side a little, gaze at the ground and nod our heads, signaling resignation to fate – while simultaneously reveling in the success we've met on the path we chose.

I smiled mildly in return, making sure my own lips covered my teeth in solidarity. I considered whether to go into detail about how the country is ripping apart at the inner seams, as our legal system further devolves into a morass of mediocrity and hypocrisy. Instead, I defaulted to my other work with cryptocurrency and Web 3.0, and then, since he's in finance, prattled on about bitcoin while we geared up in the otherwise empty student prep area.

*

AFF Level Two.

Okay.

I wasn't going to do the skydive maybe. I mean, I was going to go through the motions and ride up on the airplane with this Blue-eyed Finance Guy, sure, but I could always decide at the last minute to stop everything and ride back down and walk away from the dropzone forever.

I was in the driver's seat here, after all, it was my money and my life. I could pull the plug anytime I wanted, couldn't I?

Couldn't I?

*

AFF Level Three.

Now we were really cooking: The idea that I was about to initiate two – or, if time permitted, possibly four – ninety-degree turns struck me as out of this world.

My Irish reserve instructor was not only cheeky – *Have you read Joyce?* I asked, about to reference a short story of his that evoked my arrival at Dublin in snowfall; to which he responded that he'd started *Ulysses* but found *Finnegan's Wake* "much more accessible" – he was also cute: I liked especially the nose and labret piercings and longish-but-not-too-long hair.

And, wouldn't you it, here was the Puerto Rican again, too – on my main side. I flushed with embarrassment because of what happened last time.

You see, at the end of my Level Two jump, after I'd dragged him and the Blue-eyed Finance Guy "across the sky," canopy landing traffic had kinda wigged me out – or, rather, I'd wigged myself out – and, so, I started doing a bunch of turns – 180 degrees, 270, maybe even a 360 – under a thousand feet.

The Puerto Rican had to yell into the radio to stop turning – which, of course, I used as an excuse to turn some more, because, well, I could say that it's because I thought he couldn't understand actually, he couldn't see what I was seeing, he couldn't see the madness and imminent death before my eyes…

But, of course, that's exactly what he saw. Because of all the turning.

"Don't ever do that again," I was told.

I murmured an excuse about trying to avoid the flurry of canopy traffic, but stopped myself and swallowed my pride because I knew he was right.

Alright. Accept it and move on.

Get back into the present, the here, the now: AFF Level Three.

I wasn't going to do the skydive maybe. I was going to go through the motions and ride up on the airplane, sure, but I could always decide at the last minute to stop everything and ride back down and walk away from the dropzone forever.

I was in the driver's seat here, after all, it was my money and my life. I could pull the plug anytime I wanted, couldn't I?

Couldn't I?

Fuck.

There was the door.

If I was gonna back out, it was then.

I had one more second.

Half a sec-

There was no backing out now that we'd left.

Blackness.

What's happening?

Breathe.

Breathe.

Breathe.

Breathe...

Oh my god, the Irish guy has let me go.

Oh my god, I'm turning to the left — just like I was supposed to.

Oh my god, I'm smiling.

Turning back 90 degrees.

The Irish guy is smiling back.

Can he see me shrug? I mean, there's so much time and we're still so high up that I get to do another set of turns.

Oh my god, this sensation!

I am flying.

*

I'd see, later, watching the video, that my hands once again clenched awkwardly in the Gremlin gnarl, just as they had on my Levels One and Two.

But still.

I was moving in bodyflight.

I was turning around in freefall, thousands of feet above the planet we call home.

And no one could ever take those precious seconds of unimagined gloriousness away from me.

*

My AFF Level Four jump was a disaster.

First of all, what was up with this instructor and why was she so grave? I mean, she was hot and all, but, shit. Did someone tie invisible weights to the corners of her mouth? Aren't Brazilians supposed to be fun-loving?

She patiently went through the dive flow with me on the ride up to altitude. I humored her, and myself while I was at it.

I mean, you're with me here, right? How hard could it

possibly be – to just plummet?

To just aim my hips down in an arch, stay belly to earth, and maintain relative stability?

And be let go of in the sky, completely, for the very first time?

What could go wrong?

"Are you ready to skydive?"

And there we were: on a plane packed in with twenty other crazy people, squished against one another and sweating under our rigs, preparing to leap out in less than three minutes or so.

I smiled.

She smiled back.

Hey – the weights were gone!

That glimmer in her eyes – check it out.

Fuck yeah I was ready to skydive.

Except… I could still decide at the last minute to stop everything and ride back down and walk away from the dropzone forever.

I mean, I was in the driver's seat here, after all, it was my money and my life. I could pull the plug anytime I wanted, couldn't I?

Couldn't I?

Blackness.

Brea-

Oh my god!!

Why are we spinning?!

We are still spinning.

How in the hell do I stop spinning?!

Fuck!

Okay that's better.

Not really.

Are we still spinning?

Why isn't she letting go of me?

Why am I thinking about how much it'll cost if I fail this level and have to do it over?

I don't want to skydive ever again.

I don't want to be on this skydive.

Where are we in the dive flow?

Is it pull time yet?

I think this pull time is as good as any.

I'm going to pull.

Fuck!

Where is that goddamn ball?

Where is it...

Ok, lemme just run my hand down the side of my rig like they told me until I f-

WHOA.

I'm open.

She must've pulled for me.

Jesus Christ, look at that line twist — how the hell am I going to get out of this?

*

Mohammed the Smiling Qatari beamed at me as he donned his rig in the student gear-up area.

"What happened?" he asked, motioning his chin at the hand I was nursing with a paper towel and bandages.

Umm...

"Oh, don't worry about that," the cute Irish guy said to his tandem student, when he saw her eyes widen at the blood. "She's learning to jump alone."

The tandem student looked away — though not until after meeting my eyes and gawking a little longer.

I turned back to Mohammed, who was, of course, still smiling.

"I just fucked up my entire Level Four jump," I moaned. "I fucked up the exit, I fucked up stability, I fucked up deployment and I fucked up the landing. I think I'm going to leave and never come back again."

I raised my bandaged hand… and waited for sympathy.

"Well, if you do that," he observed, without missing a beat, "then you'll fuck that part up, too."

I faced him directly.

I chewed on my bottom lip and might've narrowed my eyelids, ever so much.

*

Regardless whether we watched the video together before or after my conversation with Mohammed the Smiling Qatari – I can't remember – the Brazilian expressed scant interest in my excuse that, once I started spinning, everything else was destined to go to hell.

"We still have the rest of the skydive," she pointed out.

I gritted my teeth, chewed on my lower lip, and probably narrowed my eyelids again.

*

All of which is to say that, one or two loads later, I was on my way back up.

I wasn't going to do the skydive maybe. I was going to go through the motions and ride up on the airplane, sure, but I could always decide at the last minute to stop everything and ride back down and walk away from the dropzone forever.

I was in the driver's seat here, after all, it was my money and my life. I could pull the plug anytime I wanted, couldn't I?

Couldn't I?

Blackness.

Breathe.

Breathe.

Breathe.

Breathe...

Oh my god.

The Pretty Red-haired Instructor has let go of me.

Wait, where did she go?

Okay. She's up there to the right a little.

Breathe.

Keep arching.

Breathe.

Oh my god.

I'm skydiving.

I am fucking skydiving all on my own.

This…

This must be what Heaven is like.

*

"Beautiful skydive, Zoe," came the Pretty Red-haired Instructor's voice over the radio, once I was under canopy.

The world spread out before me, in quietude, beneath.

*

I'd had a major line twist. But, I'd gotten out of it after a while, and, what's more, I hadn't eaten *that* much shit on landing.

I would remain on clouds for the rest of the day.

The Pretty Red-haired Instructor could tell.

"Remember that feeling," she said, as I knelt in front of her on the packing mat, debriefing the skydive and trying to put my experience into words.

We shared the moment.

Then she signed my logbook, with a gentle smiley-face reminder to breathe.

Yeah, so, whatever, the video, I'd see later, would reveal those awkwardly clenched Gremlin paws. Perhaps someday I'd relax more.

But, in the meantime, I sensed my very consciousness – having molted another layer of mind-gauze woven from the panoply of insecurities that had held me back in life this whole time – dissolving around the edges and into thin air.

*

Oh dear.

The Brazilian again. She looked slightly peaked without that luscious red lipstick today. And, was she tired or just not wearing eye make-up? Were things going to go poorly again?

"Are you ready to skydive?"

Hey, I could still pull the plug anytime I wanted, couldn't I?

Couldn't I?

Minutes later, my AFF Level Five was in the books.

*

Jesus Fucking Christ.

He was going to push me out of the airplane? When I was curled over into a head-down squat at the door, my toes over the edge, just sort of waiting, without knowing when it was going to happen?

And then I was supposed to tumble out, flipping uncontrollably in the sky for several seconds before arching, so that I could practice regaining stability, just in case — during some future skydive — I were to lose it and everything were to spiral to shit?

Everyone said AFF Level Six is the most fun... but, to me, this exercise sounded rather horrifying.

What am I doing this for, exactly?

Maybe for the palliation of whatever impulse has driven me back onto this goddamn airplane to enjoy yet another interminable-yet-way-too-fast climb to altitude, apparently?

Here we go.

Alright.

This skydive I am absolutely not going to do. I am going to go through the motions and ride up on the airplane, sure, but I will certainly decide at the last minute to stop everything and ride back down and walk away from the dropzone forever.

Because this insanity really is beyond imagining.

No one in their right mind would —

Oh shit, the door is open.

I'm not going to do this.

The groups are leaving.

I'm not going to do this.

My feet are following the instructor toward the door.

I'm not going to do this.

We are spotting the dropzone and exchanging a thumbs up.

I'm not going to do this.

My toes are hanging over the edge and I've bent my head toward my shins and grabbed my knees from behind.

This is fucking nuts.

I'm leaning forward and no longer awaiting a push — because I cannot wait to reach the point of no return.

This is happening.

I've started flipping through the sky.

The blackness has overtaken me, as usual — yet, this time, I somehow sense where my body is in relation to the ground.

I arch and feel stability set in.

The image my instructor captured at that instant would become one of my social media profile pictures for a while — my body position rendering me into a flourish of anatomical calligraphy etched above the horizon.

This landing was the first one I ever did off-radio — relying on myself for the rest of the skydive after I reached back down to that little faux leather ball, and conducted an awkwardly-clenched-Gremlin-hand pull.

*

I have a confession.

First, lemme just say, wind comprised my nemesis this entire time.

I mean, of course I'd fall in love with this goddamn sport at this goddamn time of year, right when the legendary winds of Perris started picking up for the season, thereby shutting down AFF jumps for several hours beginning sometime around late morning or noon, you know the drill, predictably unpredictable nonsense, very difficult to work with, until late afternoon.

The school had had to call us back from altitude three times so far, as the gusts awoke all of a sudden, heartlessly triggering a student wind hold, when I was right about to jump. Once, I'd been standing only a few feet from the door.

So, yeah.

My confession is this: Secretly, I felt relieved each time.

Oh, thank God — I didn't have to churn through that routine of not doing the skydive maybe: The decision had imposed itself on me; circumstances beyond anyone's control had put an end to this mad charade once and for all.

It wasn't meant to be, obviously, I told myself each time.

And yet...

As soon as I was back on the ground, I itched to get back up again.

To taste more bodyflight.

To make love to the sky.

To fly.

And, so, you see, it was motherfucking going to go this time.

This AFF Level 7 jump was motherfucking *going to go.*

We were going to motherfucking go up and get out of that motherfucking door and motherfucking skydive...

And yet...

The Tall and Lean Former Marine could tell something was wrong.

We'd been through the dive flow on the ground several times – but, I remained a little off. Maybe it was my bloodshot eyes, or perhaps the slight tremble in my hands, the crack in my voice, the half-assed-ness of my arch in the mock-up, or my oversight in skipping a piece like the initial altitude check or whatever...

He knew.

"I'll be right back," he said.

I nodded, then stared quietly into space for a while.

My heart leapt a little when he came back.

"I've pushed us back to the next load, on a 40-minute call," he explained, leading me to a practice room, hidden away in a remote corner of the dz. "That'll give us more time to set up a successful skydive."

In the moment, I did not really think about how it cost him to buy me this opportunity. That instructors get paid per jump – and therefore every missed opportunity is lost money for them – would only occur to me afterward, once my appreciation for his perceptivity emerged.

In the moment, as you've gathered, I was just relieved.

And grateful for another instructor to trust so deeply.

*

We went through the dive flow over and over again – in the practice room, where, on the raised creeper, I would arch and arch and arch, as he clasped my ankles and slowly spun me in simulations, helping me gauge how much to carve my arms left or right to initiate and stop 360-degree turns – and then, outside, at a mock-up, over and over again.

Patience pretty much oozed out of his pores.

And yet.

Don't forget: the winds.

It was around the witching hour of noon, so their predictable unpredictability threatened to pick up any minute and cancel the jump altogether.

Each second pushed us a little closer.

In the practice room.

At the mock-up.

In the loading area, as we waited.

And now here, on the plane.

As if to urge time to pass faster, you know, by filling it with something before the winds could rush in, I motioned to the stitching on his pants, and asked about being a Marine.

"Thanks for noticing," he said. "Most people just say, 'Army.'"

We sat in silence for a while.

Well, silence relative to the din of an Otter climbing to

altitude.

"Can I ask you something else?"

I was peeking out beyond that self-engrossing apprehension bubble that had bounded me all this while, trying to engage with the world rather than withdraw into the not-doing-this-skydive-maybe thing.

"When did it click for you?"

He cogitated a moment.

Then, he shared that, for him, skydiving was really more of a journey: He'd been doing this work for eleven years.

I nodded, hanging on his every word, fearful only of the point where we'd lapse into silence again.

And, when we did – in the minute or two before we reviewed the dive flow one last time – I thought: *I am going out that goddamn door this time, wind hold or not, we are going to motherfucking skydive.*

*

Back in the practice room, as the video played, I lapped up his feedback and encouragement with the same thirst as I had on the plane.

Did I do anything wrong?

I got through everything — but, had I performed each phase well enough?

Was I going to have to do a repeat?

Did my awkwardly clenched Gremlin hands betray too much apprehension?

He played the video one more time.

"Aaaaaaaaand that's a pass," he said, turning to me.

Holy shit.

I'd graduated.

Jump 10: *First Solo*

And then one day I jumped out of a plane alone.

It was just the sky and I.

Jumps 11 – 18: *Open Softly*

Oh my god.

That overwhelming blast of emotion as soon as I leave the plane is just too much.

This instant of eternity is all there is.

The pattern here – or so I thought – was predictable. Any fear would dissipate upon leaving the door, as it always had before, when, once outside, I immediately acclimated into acceptance that there was no turning back. Whatever would be embraced me, and I it, in return. Everything else fell away: any remaining panic morphed into submission to inevitability.

The blackness, you remember, in which all I could do was breathe.

And arch.

And breathe…

Until my vision returned and the world came back.

So, you can, I'd hazard, imagine my surprise on jump 11 – a second solo skydive, holy shit, an hour or so after the first – for which my logbook reads: "First time I consciously watched the plane after jumping!!!"

It may sound like such a tiny step. But, piercing the blackness bubble that had enveloped me every time I previously exited up to now caused its corollary – my sphere of awareness – to expand with light. The emergency I faced became an experience beyond reckoning: This sensation I was growing accustomed to felt like love.

*

Jump 12.

My first official "coach" jump – with none other than the reserve instructor from my AFF Level One skydive. You know. The one who resembles the first guy I ever slept with?

Yeah, that one.

Excitingly, now that my sphere of awareness had enlarged ever so much – not just in the sky, but also, concordantly, on the ground – I could at last begin to appreciate our interactions. Like, you know, let myself revel in the warmth he engendered.

I've described my first lover elsewhere as a hawk-nosed dude whose profile could have been pounded onto a coin from the Roman Empire. This instructor – let's call him the Tall and Lithe Guy With Piercing Eyes – had a longer and lighter frame. But, he was just as masculine; and the silhouette he cut against the harsh desert sun of Perris Valley smoldered similarly, aquiline and definite.

Fucking smoldered.

Blinking widely, I craned my neck to look up at him, standing before me here in the student gear-up area.

His deodorant swopped up my nostrils as he cupped his chest and lengthened his arms to demonstrate how I should track away from him in the sky – straightening my body against the relative wind so I'd shoot like a rocket in whatever direction I was facing – before deploying my parachute. It was then I realized how thin he was – how I could have traced the veins on his forearms with the ink of my saliva.

Zoe.

Pay attention.

Right. So, it'd be the third skydive of the day after my solos – assuming, of course, the wind didn't ground us.

Although, then again, maybe, just maybe, if the pilot changed the safety light from green to red and we were still close enough to the door, well, maybe neither of us would see it and we'd jump anyway. Just sayin'.

I mean, that is, if I didn't decide at the last minute to stop everything and ride back down and walk away forever.

That could still happen.

Couldn't it?

What*ever*.

The thing about coach jumps was that, having made it beyond the pass or fail portion of getting my license, the uber-expense of AFF jumps with two instructors, and the pressure of *all that*, I was now freed up to have more fun.

You feel me.

Like, enjoy skydiving.

Let it all go and fly.

Ohhhhhh shit.

I found myself smiling just thinking about it.

*

Except, you know, what was up with those awkwardly clenched Gremlin hands?

Seriously.

Was I ever going to relax?

*

Jump 13 was another coach jump – this time with the Puerto Rican again! – to practice fall rate modulation.

Starting with another dive exit – oh boy!

"Just imagine you're on a giant slip and slide," the Tall and Lean Former Marine had told me, back on AFF Level 7 – and that's what I'd been doing ever since.

And what I did on this one as well – before I stabilized and flew around trying to get to the Puerto Rican over there in the blue.

I am skydiving!

Up. Down.

Up. Down.

U… U…

U…

Goddamnit, how do I get up to him?

"Why was it so difficult at the end?" I asked, back on the ground.

"Because you were doing such a good job," he said, with a glint in those dashing golden brown fields of hay eyes of his, "so I was pushing you."

Wicked.

If only he'd told me beforehand to turn my head to the side and look up at him, thus presenting my helmet to the relative wind – heads are bigger than we think and helmets provide really wide surface areas! – rather than raise my face toward him and spill so much of that precious air right off my chin.

Maybe then I could have gotten up to him for a third time, not just two.

*

I stood up a landing for the first time on jump 14. Just, you know, landed and looked around, startled speechless that my feet had alit so softly, right in place.

Probably no one was watching, of course, since it was a solo.

Truth be told, I'd been trying to work on tracking for that jump – an exercise I'd eventually realize I shouldn't have been playing around with prior to my A-license, and probably not until *at least* another several dozen jumps after that, and, even then, only with a Load Organizer – an "LO" – who knew something about what the fuck was going on. But, srsly, it couldn't really have mattered much, since I likely didn't move more than a few feet in any direction.

Thinking I was tracking, and actually tracking any distance, were, I would later learn, two very different things.

*

Jump 15 was the first exit where I held onto the grab bar above the door and dangled outside the airplane for a couple of seconds before letting go.

Jump 16 involved playing cat and mouse in the sky with a

Girl Instructor Who Wore Heart-shaped Glasses. "I was having fun up there with you!" she exclaimed, as we watched the video.

Jump 17 marked the first dive exit where I managed to maintain eye contact. *Is there any way I can get this Brazilian to smile?*

Maybe it's my Gremlin paws.

*

Jump 18.

Okay.

Last official coach jump through the school.

How tantalizing to be *this close* to cheaper skydives without having to pay through the nose for instructors anymore.

"The skydives get cheaper as you go," the Puerto Rican had pointed out, early on, *"but that just means you'll be skydiving more."*

Whatever.

No, I wouldn't.

I was going to stop as soon as I earned my license.

You know. Just to prove to myself I could do it.

Aaaaaand…

It's the Tall and Lithe Guy With Piercing Eyes.

Hells yeah.

Back up we go.

Yes, I am ready!

A dive exit!

Some turns!

A backflip!

I drive toward him and then –

Wait.

What the fuck.

He's like…

moving up and down.

LOL.

He's thrown a wildcard into this dive flow.

And so…

Up and down I go.

Matching him.

All the while laughing into a tube of atmosphere rushing by at terminal velocity so loudly we couldn't hear anything else.

Oh, hey – check it out.

My hands.

They relax, for the first time — as if trailing through wind outside a car window — at which point my fingers open softly into air.

The LO Room I

"Don't ever do that again," he'd just relayed to me. Then, after a pause: "I wasn't watching, so I didn't see it to have any comment – but that's what they told me to tell you."

We were standing in the wind tunnel lobby, following some training – during which I'd mangled two minutes of air-time learning to arch better, remain stable, and do little ninety-degree turns – after my AFF Level 2.

The excuse I reiterated was, as you recall, omg, there were so many canopies whirling around and around, and also another student was right on my level and coming like straight at me, and…

As the words came stumbling from my lips, I knew they sounded even more bullshitty than they already were.

I cast down my eyes and trudged after Blue-eyed Finance Guy.

Down the stairs.

Across the parking lot.

Through the loading area…

I probably should give it all up right now. I nearly killed myself and probably someone else, or maybe two. Making all those low turns and stuff. I knew better than that.

Goddamnit.

What the hell?!

I suck.

I absolutely should just quit and g-

"This," the Blue-eyed Finance Guy said, flinging open the door to a dark cave lined with skydiving jump suits along one wall, and, pushed up against another, grungy couches strewn with whatever random skydivers had shown up at the dropzone this Friday afternoon, "is the LO room."

I regarded this alternate reality with suspicion.

"Hello!" everyone beamed.

I smiled widely.

"We want to keep you skydiving," the Blue-eyed Finance Guy explained.

And then he told me about what happened here.

*

The timing was perfection.

Although I'd been welcomed "home" only a few days before, due to the sticking-my-tongue-out thing, I continued to wonder whether I'd nevertheless always remain a little out-of-place in this bizarre and inexplicable wormhole, drifting about among so many military and adrenaline junkie types, some of whom – for all I knew – might be less than pleased, or at best quaintly amused, to have a free-spirited transsexual Los Angelina lawyer and weekend artist wandering around.

Indeed.

I may very well have strayed back to the cocoon of my prior life eventually, re-enveloping myself in familiarity and comfort zone certainty, had it not been for the Load Organizer room and everything I gleaned there about skydiving and the diversity of human experience and life itself, not to mention the friendships that found me within those cave walls and hand-me-down jumpsuits and skydiver banter about dropzone lore – but, also, mostly about sex – as I languished in between skydives, and through endless wind holds, waiting for the next jump.

You see, I took the Blue-eyed Finance Guy at his word and started showing up on each one of those waits, and, eventually, other times – after we'd finished jumping, or, as you'll soon learn, on a day when I didn't jump at all – just because.

Or because, I should say, in all my 41 years, I'd never felt so welcome anywhere else before.

Well. Except for maybe an addiction recovery meeting room.

I mean, think about it.

"Hi, I'm Zoe," I'd said when the Blue-eyed Finance guy first introduced me.

"Hi Zoe!" everyone cheered.

*

The Brit was a sort of gentle giant – very tall and large-framed, yet approachable and warm as a puppy. Like, if puppies could stay puppies through adulthood. Whatever. You know what I mean.

His clear brown eyes glinted almost continuously, even though the door to the LO room was normally shut against the summer heat, and there was hardly any light in the absence of windows.

Although, come to think of it, maybe there was a window, and it was covered up.

Didn't matter. Illumination came from inside, somehow.

You know.

I know you do.

"When you're done with your coach jumps through the

school," the Gentle Giant Puppy Brit intoned, in that way that only the English might do, "commandeer me for the day and we'll do as many jumps as we can together."

Jumps 19 – 26: *Other People*

The first order of business when I got to the dropzone that Saturday morning was, of course, to go find the Gentle Giant Puppy Brit and commandeer him for the day.

I mean, he asked for it.

Was I swelling with joy as we rode up to altitude, thinking about how I had finally graduated from school instruction to jumping with other people? How relieved I felt to be on a skydive where I wasn't being tested on anything? How I was just, you know, inside a plane that I was about to jump out of in the middle of the sky? Probably.

But, truth be told, there was also that lingering thing about it being my money and my life and pulling the plug anytime I wanted…

Because I don't have to do this skydive…

Nothing is forcing me out the door…

Except…

Except this urge, this compulsion, this ravenous desire to fly and…

Where the hell is he?

I mean, here we are, in the middle of the fucking sky and I'm looking all around – to the left and to the right – I'm spinning a 360 and looking up to find him – we're already at 9,000 feet – 8,000 – 7,000 – where the hell could he be?

*

"Your arch is magnificent," he declared as we parsed through the video in the LO Room.

It was true.

My AFF instructors had so thoroughly ground the position into my brain, which, in turn, had panicked an even sharper bend into muscle memory, that I was, in essence, plummeting and spilling air in the shape of a taco.

"I was chasing you and had to arch like bloody hell to get down to your level," he explained. And, indeed, the footage showed him steering and changing direction to accommodate the spins I did while looking for him – I resembled a cartoon character comedically missing whomever she was searching for – *Where the hell is he?* – by a hair's breadth, again and again, for the first 6,000 feet of a skydive.

*

What a day it turned out to be, though.

I got to practice docking on his legs and arms – *oh my God, I'm flying around this great big blue and touching someone's legs for*

121

the first time — doing dive exits — *wheeeee* — modifying fall rate — *maybe I can fly like, you know, a little less of a taco?* — holding there, in freefall, face-to-face — *holy shit, I'm staring into another human being's eyes at terminal velocity* — and, meanwhile, standing up one soft landing after another — *wow*.

What a goddamn drug this sport is.

Can I have some more?

*

A solo?

Really?

But I prefer to jump with other people now.

No one's available?

Well.

Okay.

360s then.

Pick a heading — any heading — and spin.

*

It had to be done.

I was not looking forward to it, however, there was no way around the requirement.

This truly, truly sucked.

From 12,500 feet there's some *time*, okay, you know, enough to sort out a problem.

But...

A "hop-and-pop"?

Leave the goddamn aircraft at like 4,500 feet or whatever?

You mean, the altitude where I usually deployed my main?

I get that I've gotta prepare for an evacuation in the event of a midair emergency, but, like, let's get real here.

How anxiety-inducing.

How utterly dreadful.

Meanwhile, of course, I had managed to slice open my finger while trying to help the Nurse With The Purple Hair Tips close the door on the runway before take-off.

So far, she and I had been aboard a plane together – about to do this AFF Level skydive or on that or this other coach jump – for at least three of the mid-ascent cancellations I'd been subjected to. You remember: those various aborted jumps in between me and the A-license that would mean I'd never have to sit through another student wind hold ever again.

"You," I'd mouth, exaggeratedly, whenever I saw her seated, "get off this plane!"

She'd explain our inside humor to whomever she was with, as we made hand gestures at one another, and laughed.

Laughing usually helped.

Not so much this time, though.

I examined my bloody hand, wondering if it was jumpable?

Yeah, it looked jumpable, why not.

But this mess…

Would it distract me on my skydive?

This torturous, low-altitude exit of a skydive, which already had me in knots and emotional throes, to begin with?

The Nurse With The Purple Hair Tips handed me a paper towel that the pilot had passed back.

I dabbed my wound, and, as I applied pressure to stop its gush, spent the next 2,500 feet or so wondering what the fuck.

Seriously.

What. In the. Actual. Fuck.

But then, next thing I knew, the Nurse With The Purple Hair Tips was helping me open the door, only this time I exercised some caution so as not to injure myself, and, there I was, checking my spot and waiting for the red light to turn to green and being basically like *whatever, you know, the hand is still functioning and blood is water soluble, so, it'll wash right off my handles or break lines or wherever it gets, and, you know, if I don't do this jump I'll just get back down and go back on another motherfucking wind hold and –*

The paper towel has been stuffed down my underwear and I'm out the door.

My fingers are awkwardly clenched – but only ever so much, and the Gremlin gnarl has mostly gone – and a smile has broadened across my face.

Other than those pesky fingers, revealing but a trace of tension, my body is arched, and relaxed, my hips are angling toward the earth, as the heart in my chest thirsts for everything out there…

Where I know I belong.

The image that the Nurse With The Purple Hair Tips captures in this instant becomes my profile picture for several months, and, many months after that, the Happy New Year e-card I send out to hundreds and hundreds of family, friends and colleagues.

"Best holiday card ever," one of them responds.

Well. It's certainly the best that I have ever done.

*

The Nurse With The Purple Hair Tips and I brave the odds for my two final licensing jumps.

Up we go – tempting fate the entire ascent, sharing glances like bandits trying to get away with something.

Until at last.

Finally.

She and I have prevailed against the wind holds.

We are out the door.

The first jump is a cat-and-mouse exercise where I get freaky chasing her around, and the next is one where I practice slides. "You don't even really have to move," she'd said, looking at me as she demonstrated, outside a mock-up. "Just *think* about moving to the left, and then to the right, and then to the left…"

Who would've known. Moving around in the sky has already become like moving around here on earth.

Just *think* about it…

Just *think*…

*

"The oral exam is always my favorite part."

The girl behind the counter sort of looks at me for a second – with mild surprise – before she chuckles and hands me paperwork to sign.

"You're going to fit right in," my examiner says, and motions for me to have a seat so he can start asking test questions.

*

That day, I become an A-licensed skydiver.

I walk around the dz with a bounce in my step, boasting the tradition of a blue stamp on my forehead.

No more student fucking wind holds.

If planes are going, I can jump whenever I want.

Look.

Okay, so, yes — I'd told myself this whole time I'd stop as soon as I achieved my license.

25 jumps or so would be enough, my reason and rationality said.

Anything beyond that would be nonsense, I admitted.

Yes.

True enough.

But...

What about doing one more — this time with the LOs — like, with a group or something?

So, yeah, okay, I'll stop.

Sure thing.

Right after the next jump.

The LO Room II

"So, you think I should buy it?"

The Bearded Guy With Over 14,000 Skydives freezes in the middle of folding the air out of his canopy and looks up at me, his gaze bright and alive. He pauses ever so much to lend maximum dramatic emphasis.

"*Yes.*"

Meanwhile, the Argentine Beauty fingers the leg straps that curl like ivy around my thighs and up along the curve of my pelvic bones.

A light breath escapes her lips, as if she's taking in vast wilderness or a work of art that encapsulates the majesty of human experience.

"It fits perfectly," she purrs.

"Fucking *yes*," the Bearded Guy With Over 14,000 Skydives repeats, going back to deflating his canopy.

The price is right – $2500 for a container, a 149 main, a 160 reserve and an AAD which is still good for another year. (For non-skydivers: these sizes refer to the square feet of canopy overhead; and an AAD, or Automatic Activation Device fires a reserve in an emergency, for example when a jumper has lost altitude awareness or consciousness and would otherwise hit the ground at terminal velocity, without a canopy overhead.)

This baby is ready to jump.

"I'm still on a 190," I lament. "And they won't rent me a smaller canopy to downsize yet because they say I'll break both my femurs."

"Who won't?"

"Square One," I explain, shaking my head at how much money I've already spent on rental rigs from the dropzone's on-site pro shop.

It's true, I can pack up or down one canopy size. So, this container will accommodate a 170.

But still.

I'm not quite ready to downsize to a 170 yet.

I mean, I don't want to break both my femurs.

And, I don't have my own 170, anyway. Though maybe I can find one...

"Zoe..." the Bearded Guy With Over 14,000 Skydives begins.

It's true, this rig did land in my lap.

I mean, like, *literally*.

As in, five minutes ago, I was sitting on the ratty bed-bug infested dusty couch and someone appeared with a perfectly-sized ready-to-jump rig for sale – and then, when I expressed interest, deposited it in my lap, and departed.

But, do I really want to spend $2,500 right now?

Srsly. Just wait a sec.

Do I really think I'm into this sport enough to make the commitment to buy a fucking skydiving rig?

"Yeah, you're right," I confess.

I extricate myself from a mesh of leg straps and the Argentine Beauty's hands, dash out the door and through the packing area, and across the parking lot.

My bank doesn't have a branch in the illustrious city of Perris, so it's going to take at least three or four ATMs to cobble this purchase price together.

Jumps 27 – 36: *Eye Contact*

It is my 27th jump – my very first as a licensed skydiver – and I am dirt diving a six-way with the LOs.

Feels kinda like becoming an upper classman in high school, getting to walk through a skydive like I've been watching the big kids do, over these past few weeks of wind holds and coach jumps and waiting around to break through to the other side.

The Bearded Guy With Over 14,000 Skydives – he's become a mentor to me, after our many conversations in the LO room, by now I think I've learned that he worked side-by-side with a transsexual for many years, back in the 1990s or whatever – grabs me by the arm and installs me in the door of a mock-up near the boarding area, and, rather than go through the minutia of how to exit in a chunk of other skydivers, basically tells me to relax and hold on.

Up we go.

I still don't have to do this, I probably tell myself once or twice on the ascent.

By now I know it's bullshit though.

And so, now, here I am, standing outside the door of an

aircraft at altitude in a chunk of other skydivers for the first time, watching my mentor's leg for the ready, set,

GO.

*

Heya. There are a few more six-ways, a couple of five-ways, a four-way and a three-way.

On these jumps, I'm spinning around in the blueness, trying to modulate my fall rate so I'm not flying too slow or too fast, feeling shit out and dropping into frustration and bouncing up past bliss and ecstasy, in various alternations – all the while castigating myself for being less than perfect and not knowing how to do everything already –

Except that it's such a blast, so, mostly, I forget those limitations and emotional peregrinations

and

just

fly.

Feel me?

*

Perhaps the most startling lesson – as well as the most challenging one to implement – is eye contact.

You know: that part where I'm supposed to continue meeting other human beings' gazes – oftentimes for much longer than we might do on earth – as long as possible.

As our hands are moving through the 123mph air to meet docks and grips.

As our bodies arch and flatten to move down or up relative to one another.

As we swirl around in the sky, like ballet dancers, facing each other through a turn and whirling around to complete the circle and take a grip again.

As I arch or flatten a little, each time, because I am still learning to stay level during a turn, let alone a 360.

Eye contact.

Eye contact.

Eye contact.

Look.

Pierce me through these windows to my soul.

They are open and ready for you to enter.

Come on.

Hop right in.

I'm yours.

Here.

Lemme tell you a secret.

The closest phenomenon I've experienced, with you or anyone else really, is making love.

You know, that climax of intense intimacy, coupled with the vulnerability involved in placing so much of ourselves in each other's hands.

Because that's what we are doing up here.

You and I.

Placing our lives in one another's hands.

Each time once forevermore.

Jump 37: *Worth Dying For*

A 7-way.

I dive out and find myself flying to the base of the formation, and then over to my slot.

I'm early on enough that each skydive still means a lot of firsts like this.

"Flying to the base."

Shit.

Only a few jumps ago, I couldn't have told you what a formation – let alone the "base" of one – even *was*.

*

At breakoff, I track away – straightening my body like a board, as I've been trying to do since I started jumping in groups, to achieve as much separation as I can. And I certainly need to on this jump, let's get real for a sec, at this stage, seven people are a lot to be on a skydive with.

I probably freak out a little – jittering in between get-the-fuck-away-from-these-assholes and oh-my-god-you're-hemorraghing-altitude-fucking-pull-already-you-crazy-bitch – and so I probably pitch a flash too soon, you know, while I'm still tracking, most likely — or, maybe there's another explanation that I think through when I look back on it from the future —

but hey

we're not in the future yet are we

we're right here

and

oh

fuck

line twist okay can I kick out of this OH MY GOD I'M SPINNING look red grab red peel pull look silver grab silver peel pull ARCH okay another line twist in my reserve kick out okay quick canopy control check oh shit where's the dropzone we jumped west didn't we oh fuck I have to cross the runway at 1,000 feet are there any planes no planes okay go go go alright I'm going to have to land downwind shit don't collide with anyone okay this is the first time you've ever flown something as small as a 160 Zoe don't think about it just keep the heading no time for a turn onto final stay steady stay steady okay here comes the dirt not yet not yet not yet flare flare flare slide it out . . . okay well now I know I can fly a 160 if I absolutely have to thank you God

*

Later on, I would post: *Now that the adrenaline is gone, I'm feeling a little emotional. TBH, I did not know whether I would be able to make it through my first cutaway when it hit. I went into auto pilot and the whole thing happened in a flash — literally, a flash of white light, in which my only thought was: Is there is a God? Whatever my little life may be worth, I owe it to the instructors and coaches and load organizers who drilled our emergencies procedures into my brain and muscle memory. Grace.*

*

Meanwhile, back on the ground, everyone in the LO room has heard I've had a cutaway before I even walk in the door.

I'd been delayed in trying to locate my main parachute, which, we've just learned, is dangling from an electrical line in front of the power plant across the street. In the time it took to obtain this information, the five or ten minutes that, because of the adrenalin, expanded into like a year, news of my cutaway has spread like a Southern California wildfire.

"Now you're a real skydiver," the Argentine Beauty remarks, motioning her chin at the reserve canopy bunched up in my arms.

"Jump 37, huh?" a few others observe, defaulting into stories of their own first cutaways, and possibly other related war stories.

I stand there, hugging the fabric that just saved my life.

The Gentle Giant Puppy Brit sees through the sparks in my eyes to the heart of me, which is shaken and trembling, and very humbled into diminutive bits. Like a statue of a person shattered by some asteroid-sized wrecking ball.

He doesn't even motion me to him – he simply steps closer, and envelops me in his arms.

I choke up.

*

"Why do you skydive?" I ask the Argentine Beauty, after everyone has left to get on the next load.

She gazes at me a moment from the chair she's melted into, on the other side of the room.

Outside, in between planes taking off, it's quiet.

Even more so in here.

"Flying," she says, nodding her head slightly, as if to music that's struck up on the jukebox of life. "That feeling is worth dying for."

Jumps 38 – 45: *A Jolt*

Okay so at this point it really *is* my money and my life. And I really *can* pull the plug on this thing any time before leaving the door.

I mean, it's three days after my first cutaway – a fucking *cutaway*, for God's sake, that shit was *real* – and, if I am honest with myself, I am still thinking about it.

Like, a lot.

How does it feel?

It feels as if, in that juncture, I experienced a jolt of something grander than I ever imagined or could have conceived.

A jolt.

A jolt running, from the very depths at the unfathomable center of me, to another dimension, and from the outer reaches of our multiverse, all the way back in, to the beat of my heart, simultaneously.

Fuck there was like this expansion and collapse of my consciousness – by which I mean the entirety of my hopes and fears and desires and wrath and yearning – yeah, that proverbial "my whole life flashed before my eyes" cliché – within the fraction of a second in which time shed and assumed meaning, and perception inverted and exploded outward into infinitesimal smallness and infinite largeness.

A jolt.

Fuck there was like this massive breakdown and reconstitution of my mind, through One Year, you remember, the change that required months to start yielding, taking what seemed like forever to materialize – whereas that first cutaway jolt hit and did the same thing, re-comprised my essence – *my underlying reactions themselves: my very instincts* – in a sort of spiritual Big Bang.

In an instant.

An instant of eternity.

An eternal jolt.

You know.

I want more of it.

Don't you?

I want to jump.

Feel me?

I want to fly.

I know you do.

Let's share a jolt.

Together.

I'd love nothing more.

Nor, I know, would you.

And, so, here the four of us go.

Up.

Up and away.

On another skydive.

We are out the door.

Linked arm to opposing arm in an "accordion," adjacent to one another like a human jigsaw puzzle, all looking in toward each other's eyes, at the center.

Spinning.

Linking in another accordion.

Spinning again.

Forming a circle.

Spin…

Circle…

*

That four-way is followed by another – and then comes a smattering of six- and seven-ways, and then two more four-ways.

Lots going on here – tons of shit more or less unleashing and exposing itself on each jump, here I am, trying so hard: trying to maintain eye contact, sometimes succeeding and sometimes drifting away; trying to extend my legs more and drive toward the center of the formation; trying to track sufficiently and then "stop" for a sec before deploying; trying to regain stability and rescue some of these goddamn line twists from poor body position.

It's a jumble.

*

My 45th skydive is when this baggage catches up with me.

"Your head wasn't really in the jump," the Soft Yet Edgy Brazilian observes, as we debrief the video in the LO Room.

She's right.

I was on a borrowed rig while my own was getting a reserve repack – no, of course I couldn't wait for it to be ready before skydiving again – and the damn harness felt so big, as if I was swimming around in the fucker, at some points sensing it so loose around my shoulders and chest that I wondered whether, at 7,000 feet or whatever, I might slip right out.

And yet.

Wasn't it just one jump ago that had felt so magnificent?

On that one – which I was convinced I shouldn't do because I was tired or whatever, and probably also because of skidding out into the ground on the jump prior – I'd had a Tinkerbell landing and instantly felt redeemed.

And yet.

Here I was.

Back on my ass again.

It's very confusing, this back-and-forth, this two-steps-forward-then-one-or-three-or-seven in the wrong direction.

What the fuck am I doing?

Jumps 46 – 51: *Nothing Else Matters*

Jump 46.

The Bearded Guy With Over 14,000 Skydives is our LO.

"And, remember, if all else fails," he chants on the ride up, and then we all chime in: "Improvise!"

Back on the ground, he'll comment on my awkwardly clenched Gremlin hands, sort of mimicking their gnarl as he cycles through the video endeavoring to persuade me to relax.

"I'm jumping out of a goddamn airplane!" I respond. And then, dejectedly: "I'm never going to relax on a fucking skydive."

And yet.

My logbook reads: "Felt wonderful in [the] air again. Beautiful landing. First jump back on my rig and post-Ninth Circuit argument. Floating feeling."

It had been one hell of a haul from the rock bottom of termination from the indigent defense panel in the Central District of California to the United States Court of Appeals for the Ninth Circuit – the largest federal appeals court in our nation – but, I'd made it.

I'd been fighting without relent, you remember, for what I suspect would seem self-evident to most Americans: that criminal defense lawyers, even ones who represent the poor, should operate independent of judges who appoint us.

I mean, seriously, what the fuck kind of a system do we think we have when appointing courts can strongarm defense lawyers into submission?

Especially in the federal system, where the cards are so stacked against individual rights, already?

It's just not the way things should be — let alone what our Founders intended.

And everyone knows it.

And yet.

After three years of work and preparation, there I was, at oral argument in the Ninth Circuit, stating the obvious, over and over again, to three lackeys on the bench: zombie-judges who had not even bothered to read and digest the briefs I submitted.

You think I'm being hyperbolic and melodramatic. Oh but I wish I were. One of them — there were three on the panel — actually boasted about having decided the issues beforehand — like, he literally said he had not read the extensive records I had submitted on my clients' behalf — while the others, mystified as deer in the headlights, inquired what the main issues were, yes, the very arguments I'd been litigating front and center the entire time.

Would you believe that one of these clowns even asked the prosecutor how she'd write their opinion for them?

My God. Look at these slow-witted dinosaurs sitting up there, dripping in complacency, controlling society with life tenure, and, as a practical matter, outside the scope of any meaningful review.

I mean, this level of corrosion, this disdain for our nation and our Constitution, the rights and privileges and principles that – not to grow maudlin, but it's true – men and women have shed blood and died for over the decades, the centuries of our history.

This illusion.

This bullshit.

Fuck this nonsense.

I'm going skydiving.

Straight from the courthouse to the dropzone.

Without another thought.

Skydiving.

Motherfucking skydiving, bitch.

Oh my.

Holy manifest destiny.

I feel wonderful again.

Up here, in the air.

It's my first jump back in my rig and everything is just right.

I am floating.

And.

Oh my goodness.

What.

A.

Beautiful.

Landing.

To hell with it.

Nothing else matters.

*

I refuse to leave the dropzone without one more jump.

I simply refuse.

Nothing else matters, I meant to say, a second ago, except this: one more jump.

It's a Tuesday, and, so, like, whatever — the only fun jumpers are one or two stragglers from other countries who've been staying at the bunkhouse through the week, and yours truly.

But, mercifully, a tandem shows up – and so the load sends.

Up we go.

Ready, set…

Outside, high clouds menace us with grey, and, the next thing we know, tiny ice crystals are hitting our helmet visors and pelting our hands.

Even so, my logbook reads: "Loved being in the air and under canopy."

*

Alright so the next couple of skydives are all over the place.

There's another Tinkerbell landing.

Then there's the six-way where I'm like *okay like hell this jump is ever going to come together – I'll just have a fuckin' blast with it!*

And it is on this one – we're talking about jump 51 now – when I look at the ground for the first time while I'm tracking – can you believe I've never gazed down in freefall before, I've always looked out at the horizon, or for other people, or into their eyes – whereupon a surge of love – what, love? wtf? love, srsly? for the fucking ground? – overtakes me and flows in elixir through my veins.

Jumps 52 – 56: *The Sphere*

Not gonna lie, I've chosen this canopy course instructor – at least partly – because he's cute.

His slender yoga body.

His posture.

How lithely he moves through space – as if life is a skydive.

Those murkily clear alluring eyes...

Concentrate, Zoe, you're receiving instruction on how to fly your canopy better – and you desperately need it. Remember all those crash landings in between the Tinkerbell ones! Some consistency is in order here. Discipline.

I look at him.

"Aerodynamics? Sure, I understand the basics," I lie.

It's a white lie, though – especially since I gamble he's about to go through everything I need to know anyway.

Such nice arms he has...

So nicely toned – you can see the curve of his triceps as he moves his phone through the air toward the floor in the freefly LO room (don't worry, freeflying is coming up in a second, I promise), mimicking the diagonal line downward, followed by the small lip of an upswing from a half-flare that happens, in theory, when I brake halfway, and then hesitate a sec prior to completing the movement, thereby enabling myself to step right onto the ground, one Tinkerbell landing after another.

I mean, just, really, look at those arms…

That suntanned glistening skin…

Those thick curls of hair all over his head…

"Yes, I understand…"

*

"Abysmal!"

I'd overshot the landing pattern on my first canopy course jump due to old habits, overload from new skills, and various other excuses I could pepper you with.

Whatever.

At least my logbook is honest: "Abysmal!" LOL.

For realz tho. It's on this jump, if I remember correctly, when I fly right past my target – a soft-dirt area – and smack into the packed dirt road just beyond it, and, to worsen matters, instead of PLFing – that is, performing a parachute landing fall like a normal person – I tumble onto my left elbow, you know, just basically slam the motherfucker into the rock hard dirt, as if this particular joint of mine is not delicate or angular or a very important element of my skeletal structure.

Goddamnit.

That really fucking hurts.

I should probably stop for the day.

Goddamnit.

I paid $250 for this course.

And I need to complete it for my B-license.

Grrr…

"I put you on a 40-minute call so we can debrief," the cute instructor says.

"Great!"

*

Okay so I lied to you earlier – much as I lied to the cute instructor.

The snapshot that the Nurse With The Purple Hair Tips took of me leaving the airplane for a hop-and-pop isn't from when I was still earning my A-license. It's from this jump – number 53 – the second hop-and-pop of my canopy course.

Don't @ me.

I ended up going unstable at a low altitude for that image. Because, I mean, the lengths we'll go to for killer profile pics!

Shit.

I swear on my life about one thing, however.

The bit about slicing open my hand on the door – that part really did happen.

Or did it?

You'll never know.

Anyway, such a detail doesn't matter all that much.

Because, really, who cares: on this jump, would you believe it, I get to practice flaring thousands of feet above the ground, with a paper towel wrapped around my hand, eyes closed, letting go of my expectations – along with the rear risers – to just sort of play around, *sensing* the canopy respond and *feeling* what a flare really is.

You see.

I.

Get.

To.

Close.

My.

Eyes.

While.

Flying.

As if in a dream…

I earn a good scolding for landing downwind – "Oh, my God, I could have sworn the wind sock was blowing in the other direction…" – but I kinda am all blasé because I started my flare at the perfect height, and, at least insofar as my logbook reflects, "instinctively integrated" the 180-degree panoramic and practice flares that I'd been working on while airborne moments before.

With my eyes closed.

Flying.

Flaring.

Feeling.

Dreaming awake.

*

The last three canopy course jumps – and especially the landings – alternate between "nice" and "a total fuckin' mess."

And, to be honest, my elbow does hurt.

I mean, like, it actually totally hurts.

And it's swelling.

*

In our final debriefing of the day, the cute instructor is encouraging me to try new stuff and correct my mistakes – crashing into the ground, landing downwind, flaring too soon – and glean a lesson whenever I do something wrong.

I make a note in my logbook about this whole learning process thing. You know, the ossification of the mind and how jarring and refreshing it is to break down everything I think I know and rebuild my perception of the world.

Like this whole panorama in my sphere of awareness that he's been talking about all morning.

It's true.

Thinking back, I can see now how my first few skydives occurred in a tiny bubble, albeit in the sky, wherein the only aspects my mind had room for were trying to stay stable during freefall, deploying at the right altitude, and returning safely to the ground.

But now, mega-wow, I've grown into a habit of checking the direction and strength of the wind *before* I even board the airplane, gauging who else is on the load and what they're doing and where they might be pulling, and opening myself to more of the sky and whatever is going on around me at deployment.

My sphere – which had started so tiny – continues expanding.

Within the dimensions where we perceive, as well as others, into which we intuit.

You know: the ones where we get to soar.

That elbow tho.

Man.

Ouch.

Jumps 57 – 66: *Welcome Home*

"You really should wear protective gear," she says, tight curls of glistening hair bobbing upon her forehead as she leans across the little examination room and hands me an x-ray prescription.

"Protective gear?" I chortle.

I imagine doing a skydive with, like, knee and elbow pads, and it's totally LOL.

"Yes," she nods, sincerely.

I make no effort to conceal the glimmer in my eyes.

Yeah, right.

*

My 57th jump, a six-way LO'ed by the Bearded Guy With Over 14,000 Skydives, is the first time I fly – as I note in my logbook – "softly and gently."

We're doing a waltzing spider – in which the four of us rotate grips on the Bearded Guy in the center, flying a circle around his body over the course of several thousand feet – and, even though I still have yet to maintain eye contact consistently, I do sense my hands just sort of going where they're supposed to.

Next grip is the full extent of what I'm thinking – rather than, say, modulate fall rate by arching, dig in left elbow and left knee simultaneously, maintain level – *next grip.*

Next grip.

So natural.

Next grip.

So soft.

Next grip.

So pleasant…

To just fly like this…

*

It's powerful – this high.

And – you've guessed it – I want more.

*

"Corking?" I ask.

The Kind-eyed Cameraman demonstrates by raising his hand into the air and curling his index and middle finger to resemble bent knees, descending toward the earth.

"Right, so, you're going like this in a sit," he says.

"Okay."

He flattens his palm.

"And then you belly out like this," he continues.

"Yes."

"Kablooey."

He pops his hand up above his head.

It stands to reason, of course – that terminal velocity for "freeflying" in a sit, which involves exposing less "surface area" than a belly-to-earth position (where your chest is hitting the air along with the entirety of your core and your arms and legs), would be greater – but, I hadn't really thought about it.

"How much faster do you go, exactly?" I wonder.

He widens his eyes at me.

"A lot."

Hmm...

I don my gear, contemplating the unknown, and then head over to the boarding area to become the holy terror that I will – a couple hundred jumps from now – regard with skepticism and alarm: a first-time "solo freeflier."

Look, in my defense: I *did* ask someone about it beforehand, and I *did* try to understand when the Kind-eyed Cameraman explained "backsliding." I know I am supposed to avoid that problem by keeping my hips slightly forward, as I sit in the sky, thereby engaging with the relative wind that blasts up at my lumbar region – as opposed to collapsing and leaning down, which would present the bulk of me, my torso, to a tube of relative wind that would instantly propel me backward.

But, let's be candid, what I'm really thinking is: *Shouldn't be too hard.*

Yeah, right.

Little do I appreciate then, at least as much as I would come to the more I learned, that these types of delusions are precisely what adequate group separation times for leaving the airplane are designed for.

I mean, the reality is – let's face it – I'm gonna be flailing about in various directions around the sky, unable to tell, as a "solo freeflier," with no reference point, whether I am moving, all the while struggling to get into position and hold it longer than a few seconds, at best.

What a horror show.

But, you know what, we all start somewhere.

And so up I go – and out the door.

*

"OMG," my logbook reads. "In and out of sitting – quiet rush @ one point."

It *is* the most extraordinary thing.

This feeling.

You know.

Whenever I manage to get into a sit and my velocity accelerates by a quarter, or perhaps even a third.

Just like the Kind-eyed Cameraman described: less surface area, more speed.

Speed.

A sudden *whoosh*.

As if I am a cylinder slipping into the air vacuum of a pneumatic tube, you're with me, one of those old-fashioned delivery systems in a bank or whatever.

Whoosh.

Meanwhile, my rig, which now catches force in the wedge of air between its base and my lumbar region, seems ever so loose, compared to the 56 preceding skydives, when it lay flat atop my back.

Is it going to blow off right here – in the middle of the sky?

I flail.

Zoe.

Concentrate.

Back into a sit.

Whoosh.

OMG.

This feeling.

The closest psychological experience, my logbook notes – although it's now been a generation since I've tried it – is LSD.

Whoosh.

The universe blows up into a million little pieces, each expanding to endlessness and coalescing back into reality again, shining vividly and pulsing with energy.

It's like a dream – a dreamscape spread out before me, encompassing and imbuing my senses – some dreamplace in another dimension I've always wanted to visit.

Where a part of me has always been.

Is this an emotional supernova?

Unsurprisingly, I open over a "long spot," further from where I'm used to being.

Blissfully unaware that I've most likely backslid, my instincts kick in to grab my rear risers – just like I learned in the canopy course – so that I might slow my rate of descent and nab a few more feet of horizontal distance to work with.

Because, on top of it all, I've just decided to "downsize" again.

It's my first jump on a "high-performance" canopy.

Am I gonna make it?

Yeah, probably.

Holy shit.

I'm still in the air

and

I

already

want

more.

*

I really shouldn't have been jumping – let alone freeflying for the first time – with that elbow.

I mean, the fucker seriously aches.

And, at this point, I really cannot talk away the swelling.

Looks like a big red tennis ball, this elbow of mine.

I go to the dropzone again this weekend anyway, determined to jump if I can.

Nevertheless, I do indeed succumb to being reasonable – painful though it may be, perhaps more so than the physical discomfort, if we're forthright – and nurse my wayward joint with an ice pack in the LO Room.

"The sky will be there," purrs the Argentine Beauty, as I sulk in the corner.

*

I know she's right.

Like, in my heart of hearts.

But, being grounded, even for a week, is making my blood itch.

*

Throughout the day, whenever the LO Room empties out because everyone's gotten on a load – they're all here to skydive, after all – I head out and explore the rest of the dz, which I haven't really spent much time doing ever since I drifted into the LO Room and became someone else.

"Hey, Zoe," a Nice Friend Whom I Once Gave A Hippie Tote Bag To asks, as I traipse through the creeper pad area, "do you have a tampon?"

"I'm a transsexual," I inform her.

"Oh," she responds, without missing a beat. "That'd be a no, then."

High five.

*

Later, in the LO Room, she's excited to share the tampon story – *Oh! Can I tell it?,* she interrupts, at some point.

I cannot help but remember the lady who edited the video of my very first skydive: *Welcome home.*

Eventually, she and I get to talking about her forthcoming trip to Chicago, where she's going to stay in another skydiver's trailer.

"It's such a warm community," she explains.

"Why is that, do you think?"

She ponders a moment, and then opines that it's partly because there are so relatively few of us, but also there's the thing about how, with every jump, we are putting our lives in each other's hands, ya know?

"Yeah," I nod. "I do."

*

They're really kind of beautiful, I think, studying the bones that

165

comprise my elbow.

The x-ray image lends my skeleton that otherworldly, glowing, faintly angelic hue, contrasted against the charcoal background, with light emerging from a shadow world of ether, as unexpectedly soothing as the existence of human life on a pale blue dot in nowhere.

How lovely and beautiful.

No fracture!

*

The following day, a Wednesday, I dash out to do a freefly jump. The exit is pure bliss and I spend the rest of the skydive in and out of position, naturally stabilizing into a sit at various points.

It really *is* like acid.

This feeling.

Whoosh.

But.

I am lonely.

I want to share this with someone.

So, the following day: a two-way, back with a belly organizer.

"How do you think your tracking was on that jump, Zoe?" the Sweet Retired Lady LO asks me.

"Umm… okay?"

"Do you think you got adequate separation before pulling?"

Oh dear. This Sweet Retired Lady LO is not about to let me off lightly.

"Umm… I think so?"

"How long did you track for?"

"Six seconds?"

"Let's watch the video."

And then: a three-way.

"How do you think your tracking was on that jump, Zoe?" she asks, unrelentingly sweet.

"Umm… okay?"

"Do you think you got adequate separation before pulling?"

There's really no way I'm about to get off lightly here.

"Umm… I think so?"

"How long did you track for?"

"Six seconds?"

"Let's watch the video."

I gotta admit, once again, that she may be onto something.

I need to learn how to track better. It's important not to kill myself or anyone else.

*

I can't help it.

I love my people so much.

But, I also love freeflying.

Another solo?

Itch, itch.

Scratch.

Man.

There's so much smoke in the air from the Holy Fire – the catastrophic blaze that some pyro set, apparently after threatening to do so for years on end – that it looks like I'm skydiving into Armageddon.

It is, also, the first time I am so aware of skydivers below me.

Actual human beings falling at terminal velocity – whom I can see.

This shit is wild.

Holy fuck.

Pull.

*

My eye-contact is improving.

I'm standing up or running out more and more landings.

My fall rate has started to match others' almost naturally – much like we might approach each other down on earth, gravitating together while also respecting personal space.

I'm turning more points on LO jumps where we are – to my amazement – succeeding in hitting the grip sequences we dirt dove on the creeper pad.

My tracking has improved. Really.

Really.

I swear.

I mean, my logbook even notes "watched folks tracking, while tracking."

That's an improvement, isn't it?

*

"Three hugs initiated by men today," reads my logbook. "Four!" I write, minutes later.

And to think: one of those embraces was my Puerto Rican tandem instructor. He'd read a piece I'd posted online about how skydiving saved my life: how my very first jump — with him — had meant that much.

Butterflies stirring inside me, fluttering.

Home.

Jump 67: *Now or Never*

Kinda thinking I like the 40-Or-Maybe-50-Something Contractor this much because he lacks sexual or social hang-ups. Shit is just so chill around him.

Also, he's easy on the eyes.

Though, then again, so too are many of the rest, as you've gathered by now.

I mean, the ratio of human beauty in this sport defies rationality. The dz is basically a movie set.

I'd go to bed with like at least 80% of them. Possibly 90%.

At the same time.

Zoe.

Focus.

Right.

Okay.

So, the 40-Or-Maybe-50-Something Contractor has instructed me to do some spins – 90s, 180s, 270s and 360s – to practice that modulating-fall-rate-while-actively-skydiving thing – and he's thorough to the point where we're even gonna get down on the creepers.

Hey – there's Mohammed the Smiling Qatari.

I haven't seen him since AFF Level 4.

"Mohammed." I tap him on the shoulder.

He gazes at me with those captivating almond eyes.

"You're the reason I'm here. Do you remember…"

He smiles.

"Zoe!" the 40-Or-Maybe-50-Something Contractor barks.

"Coming!"

Alright.

It's my first time on the "creeper pad," I mean, wheeling around on an actual creeper – it feels like a skateboard for my body, except one where the wheels can go in circles – as I rest my abdomen on this foam overlaid on wood, and use my hands and feet to push myself through a simulation of our skydive, relaxing into it like a yoga stretch.

First a 90 in one direction, then a 180 in the other, then a 270 in the other, then a 360…

I'm skydiving with the big boys now.

Feels like high school.

Zoe.

Concentrate.

Eye contact.

*

The dive exit is one of my better so far.

Everyone's been telling me, over and over again, until it has finally seeped in: *The head follows the eyes, and the body follows the head, so just keep your eyes where you want to go and you'll be golden.*

They were right: Eye contact really works.

On my spins, however, I do this thing where I catch and watch the 40-Or-Maybe-50-Something Contractor in my peripheral vision, rather than head on. The body follows the head, sure enough, so I overshoot my stopping points by at least a quarter turn.

And I was doing so well on the ground!

Wait a minute.

Was I?

Because, you know, I haven't told anyone, but I've been sagging into depression again.

I finished One Year three months ago.

The anger – which I'll describe shortly – has come and gone.

And now I'm in a slump.

I skydive every weekend, sure, and I love it.

But, let's get real, how long can the luster of a thrilling new sport paint over the dullness of my verve?

It's been forever since I've gotten laid.

Work is shit.

My profession, and the country in general, are train wrecks.

I'm a different person inside — *the underlying reactions themselves: my very instincts* are new — and yet, I mean, has anything in my life, insofar as it exists out in the world, actually changed?

Or, did I simply float up to the top of consciousness and stay there, where everything seemed bright and easy, for a while, in blissful, willful ignorance?

I smile on this skydive, sure.

And my hands are more relaxed than ever.

Yet my heart is partly elsewhere.

And the sadness has returned.

The cloud above.

Darkness.

*

I open to a spinning line twist. Like, spinning pretty fast.

Okay, really fast.

No!

It can't be!

Not another cutaway!

FUCK.

I will give it one second to see if I can get out of this shit.

One second.

To reach up and try to pull everything apart.

Trigger a counter-spin.

And correct.

One second.

This instant.

An instant of eternity.

*

In which I give in.

The vortex swallows me.

I embrace it without resistance.

Submission.

I can decide against cutting away, you know, I can end all this turmoil right now.

This is it, if I so choose – I'm on the edge.

And I needn't go back.

Because, if I do nothing, within a few seconds, it will all be over and I will never have to be in the world again. I will get to stop being alone, I will forget longing for love and intimacy and so many experiences I seem unable to touch, I will not have to be transsexual anymore, I will escape growing any older, I will become impermeable to being hurt or heartbroken in every way and I will go somewhere else beyond imagining, I will disappear.

Forever.

*

The second is up.

It's now or never.

Look red.

The g-force from this spin makes it difficult to move my arms.

Grab red.

Like I'm in a skyful of molasses, trying to swim.

Come on, grab red.

Like my muscles have turned to lead.

I could still give up.

Everything feels so heavy.

Fucking grab...

There's no time anymore.

GRAB RED.

The second is turning into the next.

Still give in.

This motherfucking g-force has turned my blood into drying concrete.

Still...

God?

Peel.

Don't give up, Zoe, don't give in.

Pull.

The LO Room III

"I'd much rather have an angry Zoe than a dead Zoe."

My helmet sits upside down on the scummy couch, where I've just hurled it, and everyone in the LO Room is staring at me.

"I can't fucking believe it! Another cutaway!" I wail.

The Bearded Guy With Over 14,000 Skydives places his hand on my shoulder and repeats: "I'd much rather have an angry Zoe than a dead Zoe."

I cast my eyes down at the questionable floor.

Legend has it that the carpeting was vacuumed at least once within the last few years, indeed, there are a handful of people who claim to remember the event. Even so. Yikes.

Silence.

And then the truth comes.

"I'm just so disappointed in myself."

There. I've admitted it.

The line twist was – most likely – due to poor body position. I was – probably – still tracking a little when I deployed my main.

Silence again.

"You did the right thing," a Texan pipes up from the corner. "You saved your life today."

I nod sheepishly, still gazing down at the dusty carpet.

Silence once more.

I glare over at my rig.

It glares back at me, from atop the fluffy white reserve canopy that I just rode to the ground.

Fuck.

It'll be *days* before I can get a repack and jump it again.

Jumps 68 – 78: *Kintsugi*

Jump 68. The first time I fly another person.

It's a four-way with the Bearded Guy With Over 14,000 skydives and a couple of Chinese guys who are, I gather, not all that used to skydiving in groups. Nevertheless, in our 60 seconds together in the sky, we somehow manage a few open accordions – the human jigsaw puzzle thing – and some 360-degree spins. Again I notice my hands dock without having to reach – what a feeling, being where I am supposed to, and letting the dive flow happen – meanwhile getting to help a less experienced jumper stay on level and in his slot.

Oh my god.

What a fool I've been.

The LOs have been helping me fly this entire time.

As I am doing now.

Wow.

Another first: I've tracked and then stopped.

Well, I mean, I keep plummeting toward the earth at terminal velocity, of course – but I've fucking stopped tracking and arched into position, and, as a result, am deploying in vertical freefall and experiencing what my logbook will record as an opening "like a chrysanthemum."

At last.

A soft, on-heading opening.

The world is so beautiful from up here.

*

Jump 69.

Because no early skydiving career would be complete without a Mr. Potato Head dive.

You know.

Where we chase after the LO in freefall and endeavor to insert eyes and a nose and arms and a moustache into the Mr. Potato Head she's holding out in front of her face.

This is serious stuff.

*

Jump 70… 71… 72…

I'm smiling more during skydives now.

Also, I'm maturing out of the obsession with my altimeter that has contoured my consciousness in the air up to now. But, far from losing altitude *awareness* – to the contrary – with every jump I'm gaining *more*: my mind and body are sensing, with greater accuracy, how long the skydive's lasted, how far we are from deployment, how big the ground will look by the time I need to pull.

You mustn't get complacent, I remind myself, *that's when something will happen.*

Keep your wits about you.

Jump 73... 74... 75...

All that practice and effort have not been in vain. The naturalness of these many pieces coming together, assembling, bit by bit, starts to feel like silk: I think "go over there" or "down" or "find the dock," instead of getting hung up on the technicalities of any specific movement. I simply move. Sorta like I get around back on earth: without considering how.

Also, I'm no longer crashing into the ground as much.

Holy shit.

Landing is becoming fun.

And, oh, hey.

The wind tunnel.

I mean, it's expensive, but...

Maybe it'll help my freeflying to do a few minutes on my back.

Because what the hell.

So, here I am.

Floundering.

Spinning around on my back trying to pop up into a sit.

And failing miserably.

Minute after overpriced minute.

Here in the tunnel.

Wanting to just qui–

Oh, hey.

Check that out.

There it is.

A sweet spot.

Right along my spine, near the bottom of my scapulae.

Wow.

That's so killer.

My lats have turned into wings.

I *feel* the air.

Holy shit.

I'm flying up off the net.

Up up up.

Looking up.

Fuck.

I want to put this in the sky.

And backfly gazing heavenward...

Into the blue above.

Jump 76... 77... 78...

For the first time, I pitch and look down and wonder: "Where the fuck am I?"

I'm like sitting here under canopy above some random residential area or whatever.

Laughing to myself as I imagine what people below might think if they knew.

Zoe.

Concentrate.

Alright, that's enough, srsly, where's the dz?

Would you believe it, I ride my rear risers the entire way back into a landing pattern – exhausting my upper arms with the strength it takes to flatten the angle of my canopy and retard its descent rate – somehow managing to stand up near my initial target.

There are more and more of these "redemption" landings,

which follow ones where I thump my tailbone or otherwise eat a massive pile of shit.

I'm starting to improve.

To enjoy this journey.

To love being a-sky, and then alighting back on earth.

*

How can I describe this transformation?

Any words I may grope for – they seem inadequate, woefully so, and fall short.

It's like a first love, except when we're grown up.

This baffling splendor.

It's blowing my mind.

Apart.

The fissures in my thought.

They're widening.

Like an ongoing insight, coming in waves.

A showering of perception that stops you in your tracks.

Lifts you up into dreams.

And spreads light.

You know.

I know you do.

See.

There's this inflation.

So much empty space.

Like the sky.

In between the ideas and visions and feelings and experiments that comprise us.

Where we expand.

Along with our sphere of awareness.

And then we break into minuscule pieces.

Quadrillions.

A cosmos of fragmentation.

Where once there was nothing.

The multiverse disperses.

Leaving infinity behind.

Exploding.

Faster than speed.

All in an instant – this instant of eternity.

The same instant in which everything comes back together...

Remaking us.

Reconstituting who we are.

Melding countless shards back into one.

Like Kintsugi.

The Japanese art of lacquering broken pottery.

You know – with liquified gold dust.

Whereupon afterward, those glistening lines, like wrinkles on a face, allude to lifetimes of stories: the mystery of whatever happened: an unknown past.

A sequence of broken hearts now mended.

This juncture in reality, where dreams may coalesce.

Rendering the pottery – rendering us, our conceptions of the present – ever fleeting, and more precious.

Continents of consciousness materializing in seconds, drifting back together in timelessness, yet without hesitation.

A world ravaged by the savage magnificence of its own creation.

Bathed in light.

Skydiving.

So transportative, so unforgiving.

There is such beauty in this beast.

In whose arms I seek softness through abrasion.

A first love, but a tough one.

The danger and allure of the unknown.

Eroding away the very edges I ventured into.

Gently lacerating me.

Splicing the person I was.

Editing out pieces I no longer need.

Putting me back together again.

My Humpty-Dumpty soul.

This collage that I am.

Skydiving.

It's changing me.

Jumps 79 – 81: *A Skydive by Moonlight*

First things first: two daytime jumps to familiarize myself with a new dropzone.

I've never been here before, so, of course, I have to find out what this place looks like from above, and learn where I can land.

You know, just in case…

*

Another day flashes by.

Time at the dz seems to go faster than anywhere else.

Not gonna lie, tho: I'm rather apprehensive about what's about to go down. I mean, really.

*

The sun has started to creep behind the Elsinore Mountains, showering them in blueish-gray. Grasping rays linger, dancing on the lake's surface, at the end of the runway.

Twilight is here.

*

"Death perception" – LOL.

The Smiling Brazilian, an instructor who gives us our mandatory pre-jump briefing, has this accent that causes him to explain how skydiving at night changes "death perception" – instead of "depth perception"– and the room, crammed full with 30 people, bursts into a laugh.

During our gear check at flight time, one guy is so nervous that he sputters something about forgetting to reset his AAD; a minute later, once we are all inside the little airplane, he bails back down the step ladder, and I guess that's that.

The Smiling Brazilian points out the target landing area – three car headlights on a strip in between the main and backup runways – at various points on the way up to altitude.

Three car headlights in a sea of black: That's where we'll be headed.

Jumping into blackness.

Wow.

Our ascent takes forever because we are in a single-propeller aircraft. Lake Elsinore shimmers below in the moonlight, and the ten of us teem wide-eyed inside.

The five big men go out one by one on our initial pass, and then we circle around for another to accommodate us smaller folk. I am to be first from our group because, at 1.1, I have the heaviest weighted wing load (meaning I'd probably go down fastest).

This flight is louder than I'm used to: I'd been so busy duct taping lights to my body beforehand that I neglected to put in my earplugs. But, no worries, I forget to notice the noise very early on, preoccupied as can be with charging up my altimeter by flashlight, so it will glow in the dark.

Maybe once or twice I think "Zoe, what in the HELL are you doing?!"

Yet the world twinkles so beautifully below, and the mountain-shadows stand so starkly against the moonlit sky…

Mostly I feel excitement. Maybe euphoria.

Feelings I have never known and may never experience again, you know: the splendor of a first time – the frequency of which I've missed so much, you remember, as I grow older.

Even so, what is happening hits me as the safety light turns to red and the Smiling Brazilian rolls up the door.

I take position and point out the three car headlights 7,000 feet away and take a deep breath.

Then the safety light turns green.

I hesitate for a split second – for the first time since my AFF Level 1 –

Just, you know, the wispiest split of a second –

But, then I see the Smiling Brazilian's thumbs up, and we make eye contact, and whatever is out there pulls me into it and all in this instant – an instant of eternity – I am plummeting through darkness toward terminal velocity at 123mph.

The abyss of night dilates into a wormhole where time bursts open – if I must fail to describe it, all I can say is that I feel as I imagine I might if the earth were to slow in rotation, such that gravity would operate on waterfalls to cascade diagonally – and, second after precious second unfolding, it is glorious beyond words or even thought.

My very pores imbibe a world of surroundings – as far as the eye cannot see...

Just kidding, dude, you can totally see hella shit under a full moon, as you know...

And I am startled and dazzled like I have never been before in my entire life.

I deploy at 3,500 feet and yet it still feels like the longest canopy ride I've ever taken.

I soar to my landing pattern, then soar and soar some more.

Over the dropzone, toward the charcoal mountain-shadows, through the warm invisible air...

And then, the next thing I know, I am standing on the ground, in a beam of car headlights.

FUCK YEAH, I squeal – at the top of my lungs.

FUCK.

YEAH.

*

"That's ridiculous," the Broad-shouldered Former Marine admonishes, in that mouthwatering southern twang his words drip with.

Those eyes of his glisten in the light cast from raw bulbs over the packing area.

Night hugs us.

"Always leave the party when you're having a good time," I wink. And then I'm off.

He kinda had a point tho. I probably should've done another.

But, you know what? Why chance ruining spectacular?

I'll save my second night jump – the other one I'll eventually need to achieve a D-license, down the road – for another time.

Jumps 82 – 99: *A Giant Television Screen of the Earth*

God how I love diving out of an airplane.

Jump 82 is the first time I fly without thinking about it.

By jump 83, I note in my logbook, "It really is starting to be intuitive: looking/fall rate/location adjustments."

God how I adore being under canopy.

84... 85...

On jump 86, I do a waltzing spider around the Sweet Retired Lady LO, and, in the middle of our jump, I look over at her body mid-sky, sensing, in that instant of eternity, that she is levitating right in front of me.

Whoa.

Am I in a dream?

87...

Oh shit I'm late for my dirt dive with the Sweet Retired Lady LO because I've been talking to the Slender Crypto Girl – she follows me on Twitter because a friend was like *OMG a skydiving crypto fiend: It's your twin!* – and we like couldn't shut up about crypto and skydiving.

Look. I'm sorry.

I couldn't help myself.

See, ever since I discovered the packing area where the freefliers congregate – there's a veritable Swarm of Freefly Boys over here – I've been spending less time in the LO Room.

I didn't mean to.

Not exactly.

It's just that, a couple of weeks back, I was passing by here and some Young Turk – a truly head-turning specimen of humanity, built like an inverted giant sequoia tree, mind you – remarked on my white eyelashes.

You know.

My right upper eyelashes, which, unlike any other hair my body produces so far, are white, as they have been ever since one random day in college when they changed overnight.

"I have that, too," he confesses.

"Really?" I remark, promising myself that *this time* I will start paying closer attention to men.

I mean, it's really not fair that they get to notice everything – absolutely every fucking little thing – while I remain oblivious.

I peer at his face.

Jesus.

He's a work of art.

Hmm…

I think I maybe like this area?

More than anywhere?

Oh shit I'm late.

88…

89…

I'm freeflying again!

With an LO!

And I even hit a sit a couple of times!

It's the day of the Brett Kavanaugh hearings and I want to throw up whenever I think about what our country has descended to.

This icky feeling.

This disgust.

And yet.

Meanwhile, here I am at the dz, surrounded by maleness.

Like the Young Turk – with those eyelashes.

And the Anvil – a military guy perpetually in opaquely reflective sunglasses, whose back is literally a triangle – with whom I got to talking the other day about One Year. After listening intently for like twenty minutes straight, angling his ear back for our conversation whenever he swung his formidable body to the edge of the packing area, where he expectorated another mouthful of spat, he'd encouraged me to go ahead and share the project because it could "help a lot of people." He came up and hugged me the following day, throwing his arms around me as soon as I appeared in the freefly packing area, in a hug tighter than any I could remember. Mmm…

And my AFF Level 1 reserve instructor – who, you remember, resembles the first guy I ever slept with – with whom I likewise find myself in a hug, blanketed beneath the deep voice of his "sweetheart" in my ear.

And this LO's facial bone structure – his angular jawline, his bristly stubble – and the hair on his arms and legs…

I mean, the dz is literally bursting at the seams with masculinity.

There are men everywhere.

But especially here, among the Swarm.

Fuck. I feel confused and overwhelmed.

I think I maybe like it here?

90…

Hey! The Anvil and I talk again.

He's going to become a true skybrother, this one.

91…

More freeflying!

With an LO, no less!

92… 93…

Solo freeflying…

Rolling with it…

And noting, in my logbook, that I've "started enjoying being in the air but could really *let myself enjoy it more…*"

Like…

OMG…

It really and truly is just like sex, in almost every way, isn't it.

Let go…

94…

My first two-way freefly with another fun jumper.

Of course he's cute.

"OH MY GOD!!!" I note.

95…

Another freefly jump with another LO.

96…

By this solo freefly, I memorialize, I've become "hyper-aware of safety" – by which I mean that I have *finally* begun to maintain a west-facing heading, so I'm not backsliding up and down the jump run and thereby endangering myself and others.

As my sphere of awareness expands another increment with every jump…

97…

The sky van door opens up before me and –

It's

a

giant

television screen

of

the earth.

Just fucking look at that shit.

I jump out into it.

Whoosh.

Holy mackerel – I've adjusted immediately into a sit.

In which I'm like whoa.

What

a

rush.

This

visual

is

OMG.

98…

Fawning over the sit.

And, hey – that sphere of awareness? It's out to where I register the skydiver who jumped before me.

He's too close for comfort.

Pull, Zoe.

Now.

99…

Solo freefly…

"Fuck yeah moments," my logbook reads.

Fuck yeah.

What happened exactly, you may ask?

I'll never tell.

Because… you know already.

Feel me?

Feel.

The.

Air.

Jump 100: *Naked*

"Whatever you wanna do, it's your 100th, girl."

The Slender Crypto Girl tugs on her vape.

"I wanna do it naked."

Before I've even completed the second syllable of "naked," she nods understandingly, blue plumes of mist escaping her nostrils and billowing from her lips.

*

"Can you hold these, please?" I ask the Husky Dude to my right.

He stuffs my shorts – which I'd donned over my leg straps when boarding the plane and yanked off a few seconds ago – into a pocket in his cargo pants.

He probably makes some sex joke or something.

Skydivers are like that.

My chest strap covers my small boobs in a thin blue line, stretched right over the nipples.

I've never been undressed in an airplane before.

"Fuck, now I wanna do it, too."

And thus the Slender Crypto Girl slips her arms, and then her head, out of her sports bra – which she then stows in her leggings – all without removing her rig.

She's so hot.

The Husky Dude's hot also. And, lest I forget to mention, he's not wearing a shirt, either.

I wonder if he has a boner.

Okay.

That was cute.

I'm standing here in the airplane, waiting for the first group to leave the door, and he's just slapped my bare ass.

This is serious stuff, alright.

Out we go.

*

The last time I experienced anything like this phenomenon was when I dove into the swimming pool in New York, after having returned from sex change surgery in Thailand. About six weeks had passed since the operation, so I could at last get in the water again. You remember: It was the dead of winter – a couple of weeks into January, and deathly frigid outside – as all shame washed away with the cool water rushing over every square millimeter of my body, granting me the sensation, for

203

an instant of eternity, of awakening in a dream, like the universe I'd run from this entire lifetime had collapsed into a pure and unadulterated joy of being – the peak of ecstasy, an escape hatch: Whereas before I'd been hiding, after all these years, after everything that's happened and which I may have missed, no matter, I am free.

The warmth – blasting up from the desert in late September – similarly envelopes and liberates me – my heart wells up and my mind and my spirit dissipate into this moment –

The Slender Crypto Girl and I are flipping forward and backward at terminal velocity – playing around and tumbling through the sky –

It's so extraordinarily natural –

We are feeling the air on our bodies –

And our bodies on the air –

Melding –

Dissolving –

Integrating –

The secret's out:

I

can

no

longer

tell

where

the

sky

ends

and

I

begin.

Oblivion

"His idea was that consciousness is intrinsically compelled to grow, and the only way it can grow is through strife, through life-or-death confrontations."

– Carlos Castaneda, *The Art of Dreaming*

Anger

(Months Thirteen – Fifteen; Jumps 10 – 67)

Perhaps the steam had been accumulating the whole year, and I didn't notice because I remained so focused on all the good things. Perhaps it came from the same source as the postpartum depression that so often follows birthing a creative endeavor – the very process I'd been through on other books, big cases, travel, love affairs – you know, a project you invest yourself in completely, and then, one day, it's over.

Perhaps there is no explanation. Or, perhaps there is, and I simply do not want to admit it.

The anger that overcame me in the wake of One Year distinguished itself from any other I'd known. First, this ire was just so strong and persistent. I felt furious as soon as I woke up in the morning, and then more and more throughout the day. My wrath swelled and burst without warning, infusing the world I perceived with such negativity – the polarity of everything I'd striven to make my life into – and I tumbled into sleep pretty much every night in resentment.

I was angry that One Year was already was over.

I was angry that, after all had been said and done, I felt worse and not better.

I was angry that I no longer saw anything to live for.

And I was angry that I had bothered to continue living, at all.

It wasn't supposed to be this way. It was supposed to be a really nice period. A sort of vacation following the daily exercise I'd engaged in, every morning, without fail, for an entire revolution around the sun.

You know, a reprieve.

That expectation was, I suppose, at least one cause of the problem. Little can ruin bliss more effectively than preconceived notions – and the best laid plans.

Fire and brimstone.

Rage.

KABOOM.

Second, there seemed no way out of this chasm of flames that engulfed my consciousness. Simply being angry made me angry because, if there is anything I detest – and there is only a handful of things – it's being angry. All I have ever truly cared about in life has been love, my relationships with family and friends, art and creativity, the United States Constitution, and contributing to society however I can. The pursuit of sex, success, stability, recognition, and other such fleeting palliatives or illusions have been, and always will be, a yearning for love.

And yet here I was.

Past the end of a project to save my life –

A project that had brimmed with beauty every day – some more so than others, but each glistening as special and pristine –

A project that had transformed who I was from inside out, from my very instincts to the manifestation of physical being I had become in the world, and above it, flying –

A project that turned me into a different person, opened up the world to me and me to the world, thereby changing literally fucking everything –

Or so I thought.

*

Had my survival hinged on self-deception?

Was the universe even harsher and crueler and more pitiless than I'd imagined?

Could there be any worse betrayal?

213

What was the point of healing, if it only meant feeling worse, afterward?

*

So, now you know.

Such was my frame of mind from around the time I did my first solo skydive – a few days after completing One Year – up to my second cutaway about three months later, when, as I've already admitted to you, the cloud of depression had drifted back overhead.

Can you forgive me?

I was telling you the truth about all those skydives and the majesty and transformation and what was going on that whole time and how extraordinary the summer became.

It's just there was another side.

The side that needed a jolt.

To remember.

To save me from myself, and salvage my own wild and precious life – be it out of resignation or mere default, no more than one heartbeat, one thought, one second away from giving in to the power that nearly won.

That g-force to which I might have succumbed.

214

And would have done, had there had not been this desire, this compulsion, driving me to keep jumping and dreaming – the activities I've come to live for, and scarce else – so that we might now share the next part of this story, together.

Light

Okay, Zoe.

Get back up.

Dust yourself the fuck off, and get back at it.

Enough moping. Enough self-pity. Enough torpor and complacency and indignation and superficiality and entitlement. Enough is enough.

*

I'd first learned about Eye Movement Desensitization and Reprocessing (EMDR) therapy several years before, through a discussion with a couple whose son had survived one of the worst tragedies conceivable.

"Nobody knows why or how it works," the wife explained. "But it does."

She nodded at me convincedly.

I tried to imagine how reliving trauma as your eyes follow light sequences darting back-and-forth on a screen or an LED panel could be effective at anything – let alone resolving profound psychological problems, and especially severe, otherwise treatment-resistant ones, at that.

I mean, sure, I appreciate my mystical side and have

participated in a range of edgy, tribal, spiritual shit – you've read about the dancing – although, let's be honest, were those experiences truly manifestations of higher communion? Or, were they, rather, accidents of brain chemistry, laced with breathing modulation and the pleasure of movement and human contact, collectively lulling my senses into a tranquility too easily mistaken for connection with the cosmos?

I mean, really.

Wasn't it just recapitulating bad stuff while watching light move?

*

I feel like I must've stumbled upon EMDR a few years later – in an article online somewhere maybe – in the context of cutting-edge treatment for PTSD-afflicted veterans. Apparently, I learned, the technique has helped many of them.

Sometimes it takes once to get interested.

Other times I need repeated exposure.

Or to get hit upside the head.

*

Pretty sure a friend from dance class mentioned it around this time, as well.

You know, one night, when we were covered in sweat at

the Russian & Turkish Baths.

*

Alright.

Why the hell not.

*

And, so, there I sat, planted in front of a desktop screen, holding my head still, as my eyes tracked light sequences moving to the right, to the left, to the right, to the left, right, left, right, left, right, left... thinking and talking myself through every trauma I could remember — from the childhood sexual abuse to the sexual assault as an adult to the car accidents and near misses and disastrous dates and co-dependent relationships and painfully embarrassing memories and everything nasty or unpleasant that remained for the dredging.

This process wore on for several days.

Maybe a week, even.

After which I was like whoa.

That was pretty intense.

*

Yeah so there's this one hypothesis — that EMDR helps because the activity simulates Rapid Eye Movement in the vivid dreaming phase of sleep, except a version in which we can, while awake, consciously process and work with the material.

And there's another – that the movement of our eyes going back-and-forth sorta blends the brain's hemispheres, integrating thoughts and feelings and harmonizing dissonance and easing discomfort.

Maybe like hypnosis.

Conscious breathing.

Counting sheep.

Any fucking method of repetition.

Plain old relaxation?

Sleep?

Whatever.

I'm bastardizing the hypotheses anyway.

Point is this.

I *did* feel better.

And, I liked how I felt.

So…

You guessed it.

I wanted more.

*

Oh, fuuuuuck.

What happens if I try this shit with good stuff?

And thus I EMDRed my way through One Year, working backward from my final entry, one day at a time, to the very first.

And then back up, from the beginning to the end, reliving and integrating every day in turn: each of those moments, one by one, that had made life worth living – only the gems, as you know, and nothing else – for an entire year.

The project, I began to see, had matured from a one-item daily chore into a recipe for the art of life: the aspiration to create any given day anew, molding experiences sheened with luster beyond conception, each nanosecond bristling on some unthinkably delicate, and perfect, human-sized paintbrush in the hand of God.

*

Euphoria.

More.

*

What about...

my body?

Can I incorporate, like, my feet and my hands?

And thus it was that I started using the foot massager during EMDR sessions – sorry to say, that contraption didn't really stick – and then Baoding balls: those silver Chinese spheres that jingle, ever so faintly, as you roll them around in your palms.

If only I could tell you *how* the act of manipulating my fingers into undulating revolutions creates mind and body energy that somehow chips away brainplaque, clearing pathways for thoughts wherever they wish to go, breaking through awareness and reemerging in geysers.

Or.

Whatever.

I don't care.

The explanation, if there is one, doesn't seem to matter.

After working with the Baoding balls, whenever I type shortly thereafter – journaling or making notes or working on this project or the like – my fingers dance over the keyboard.

Light as feathers.

Itty bitty wings.

Lifting me up, ever so much.

To where…

I want a little more…

*

Holy shit.

What happens

if

I EMDR

my motherfucking *dreams?*

Dreamclusters

So.

I have another confession.

There is a dreamlog, and it's been ambling along in tandem with us this whole while.

Please don't think – not even for a second – that I was trying to deceive you in keeping this other little secret. It's just that, even if I had appreciated the import of dreams at first, or how they would interweave with life in the sky, I still lacked language to share them with you.

In the beginning, you see, the dreamlog simply recorded nonsensical tidbits – whatever frayed dreamthreads I could manage to claw back from under sleep's shroud. It was only later, ever so gradually, as my dreaming practice developed, that what was initially a rote chronicle flowered into something more: a mirror reflecting beyond events and themes here in the Waking – that is, this sensory version of the world we condition ourselves to perceive – all the way to the Dreaming – that is, a threshold interspace where we get to encounter dreambeings and aspects of reality from other dimensions and nonlinear time.

(Dreambeings are what I call presences in the Dreaming. For me, they may originate in either the Dreaming itself or Elsewhere; and they periodically manifest as corollaries of people here in the Waking – like you and me. Sometimes, though, I've found, troublemakers or foes try to trick me by disguising themselves as one of us.)

I happened to start dreamlogging over a year-and-a-half *before* One Year commenced. Almost *two full years* before, actually, if I am honest with you.

Which I want to be.

I long to tell you the truth. It's just sometimes getting there takes a while.

You know.

Like when you're in love.

And you only find out who you've fallen for afterward.

When it's too late.

Are you with me?

Come closer.

*

During the gestation period – from a few weeks before the Carpenter and the legal profession broke my heart forever in the span of like three or four days, to nine months later, when it finally dawned on me that my world had caved in – during that tumultuous gestation period, my dreaming practice might only be described as a brainflush.

You see, over the four decades I had been alive so far, laziness and fear had toppled me into the routine of disconnecting myself from the Dreaming as soon as I awoke. Nervous about what I might see if I looked, I instead squelched my dreams and endeavored to relegate them to sublimation, where, of course, instead of dying off, they backed up in my psyche's intestines, festering, collecting grime and sprouting foulness and growing into an ever more rancid and unwieldy monster.

All my life up to then, I now suspect, the Dreaming Me had been calling for my attention, screaming, crying out and desperately hurling dreamthreads into the Waking, in hopes that I might catch a loose end and follow it, braving the labyrinth to see what lay within.

But, other than a handful of dreams – my first sex dream when I was 12 (sucking The Cure lead signer Robert Smith's dick); the first and second time I dreamdied (initially by plunge over a cliff when I was 18, and, subsequently, by gunshot five years later – both heralding life changes); one particular flying dreamsequence a few years ago, in which I soared through the night sky to my heart's content; and two others, around the same time, which involved similarly-feeling, but visually distinct, dreamplaces (one a familiar cave tunnel to somewhere safe and another a warm sea in an archipelago where I could swim indefinitely) – other than this handful of dreams my brain wakefully retained, I generally emerged into the Waking without much recall of where I'd just been.

Or that I'd been anywhere at all, frankly.

Yeah so I elected this whole while, instead, like most people, I guess, to wake up and promptly ignore everything I'd dreamed, to forget every detail immediately, suppressing the other worlds I'd seen like society trains us to do, without delay, the instant our eyes fly open and we face the pressures of work and making money and check our phones and bludgeon ourselves with news and images of birthdays and vacations and weddings and anniversaries and nights out and beach days and perfect children and ideal partners and other rivers of bullshit.

Not to mention, you know, whatever else the day brings.

And, so, when I finally did engage, a lifetime of backed-up dreams came exploding right out, covered in sludge.

One after the other.

Night after night.

For months upon months.

*

They usually appeared in clusters.

Dreamclusters.

Sometimes the phenomena occurred two or three nights in a row, but, normally, they spread out a little, like over a week or so.

There were work anxiety dreams. There were intergalactic and contemporary American civil wars. There were being-in-the-wrong-body-again nightmares, and, from time to time, horror shows featuring politicians – in one instance, the president presided over dinner in the form of a grotesque monster-being with a giant, bloody, rectangular, featureless head – ruining the joy of life and generally fucking things up, just as they do in the Waking.

Not to be forgotten, meanwhile, there were infestation sequences. These unpleasant affairs – revealing themselves outwardly, through cascades of bugs, or inwardly, via overwhelming sensations of feeling frumpy, dirty or grungy – caused my dreamskin to crawl.

I mean, who needs this shit.

No wonder I was ignoring it before.

There were violence and gunfight dreams – sometimes evolving into one of the full-blown intergalactic or contemporary American civil war conflicts I just mentioned, but other times involving only one asshole or a small group of brutes. The saving graces in these confrontations, if any could be discerned, had to do with finding – or, rather, accessing – power to defend myself and neutralize assailants.

And how could I almost forget the disaster dreams. You know – the Armageddon-like incidents or other such end-of-the-world scenarios, which, for whatever it's worth, normally incorporated boulders: like when beautiful Malibu fell into destruction, as enormous stones tumbled down from the flaming Santa Monica Mountains above.

Look.

I mean, it wasn't *all* hell.

From time to time, these nerve-wracking self-preservation themes and impending exigencies did, graciously, intersperse with more lighthearted stuff. Like sex with men and women alike, and also celebrity cameos, and, periodically, combinations of the two – for instance, the one where I made out with both Tom Cruise and his former producing partner Paula Wagner (she was a better kisser than he).

And, lest I neglect to mention, every once in a while I

dreamed of Las Vegas – or places that felt like Vegas – a city I'd visited in the Waking only twice so far, most recently to rock climb that fucking 750-foot mountain face in *Month Nine: Love*.

*

Okay.

Deep breath.

The point is this: Maybe the Dreaming resorted to such extremes – coloring its messages in the hues of strife and peril – because it had been trying so hard to get through to me, and for so long.

After all, we were just getting to know each other, the Dreaming Me and I, the Waking Me – but, wait: Am "I" not both? – despite having slept together our whole lives.

You know.

Like when you're in love…

*

Oh.

Hey.

Yeah.

There's this one thing.

Very early on, the second entry my dreamlog notes, I got to fly.

How could I have known what that dreamflight – and all those that were to follow – foretold?

Dreamclusters Converging

The skydiving dreams started when I started skydiving, and, now, as I write these words a year later, they continue unabated.

At one point, I took a nearly eight-month dreamlog hiatus – it lasted from the second half of One Year through the first two months of *Anger*. The first dream I recorded after this break was, you guessed it, a skydiving dream.

I needed to cutaway. My deployment bag had come out of the container and was just flapping overhead, with the main canopy stuck inside – a "bag lock" malfunction, yikes.

Also, I had pitched late, for whatever dreamreason.

Egad: a horror show.

My reserve came out in slow motion, and I slipped into an uncomfortable calm. Gazing down, I found myself over residential hills, much like the sparsely populated desert humps surrounding my home dropzone.

The jump number I was on in the Dreaming – 48 – was the same one I had reached in the Waking. And, what's more, at the time, I was (physically) back in New York – a place that usually absorbed me into seemingly dreamless sleeps, even after I had started engaging with the dreamlog.

*

To be sure, as it progressed, my dreaming practice often still featured the single-themed dreamclusters I was telling you about before.

There were sequences with lots of strangers, and a few other celebrity ones. There were several irrational-fear-of-having-bad-breath dreams, which are always particularly irksome because they interfere with social dreaminteractions or instances of potential dreamintimacy with dreambeings.

There were child and dog adoption dreams, and dreams in which I got to help people, like homeless folks or Justice Sandra Day O'Connor, who stood at an intersection unaware of her destination, due to Alzheimer's.

There were rambling house dreams, where I was in either a home that was mine, or possibly mine-but-also-not-mine, or maybe even a property that belongs to the Dreaming – and where I would discover heretofore unknown rooms, entire wings of abodes, hidden away behind a trap door or an illusory wall or some other twist in the thread of reality, a wormhole.

And, every so often, there was Vegas.

But, to get back to my point: the skydiving dreams.

They seemed to cluster more frequently, and with greater intensity, than any other aspect of the Dreaming.

Indeed, there came a week, right after my first freefly jump, when I dreamed about skydiving every night for a whole week straight. In one, I kept enjoying freeflying after my deployment altitude. In another, I flew over a forest dreamplace – the river below felt inherently familiar from another dream – and opened low, whereupon my deployment bag went into a tree, and I pulled my reserve.

(Look, I'm not saying that my skydiving dreams adhere to physics – only that I have them.)

In the final installment of this cluster, the Middle East turned into one giant dropzone, and the sense that men from my past were there crept up on me.

*

Two months later, a week-of-skydiving-dreams happened again.

Cutaway dream – regained consciousness under canopy – spinning – right end cells not opening – chopped it with listless resignation, like on jump 67. Very low by now. Landed in some sort of country club / restaurant — searched and searched for my main and d-bag and pilot chute stuff, some of which had landed in a lake / ocean that was dark but also had light from the sun somehow. Found various wads of cash — 100s in a spot near a door — felt guilty. Asked a lady if the money was hers but she said no, so I smiled and stuffed it in my pocket.

*

I mean, I'm not gonna tell you there was like some bright line, you know, where I was experiencing single-themed dreamclusters, and then, suddenly, one night, the individualized clusters converged.

Because it didn't happen that way. The process was gradual.

But then it snowballed.

Version of a rambling house dream I've had before, only I lived in this one with tenants. Rooms I didn't like — painted grossly, like my LA house when I first moved in. Pipes bursting, water coming. Small fix.

But then the entire neighborhood — quasi-Mullholland Drive — got it — and the earthquakes started. Houses crumbled to the ground, washing away. A few people flung themselves from windows.

Escape.

Tried to dreamcall my wallet and phone — which I'd left back home — through dreamspace, with my hands. No dice.

Ran into a college friend who looked old and said: I've run from here to DTLA – don't worry, I'll be fine. *Headed down a canyon path toward DTLA, or wherever, behind two guys – police in SUVs came up and stopped to talk to us.*

At one point: a mentally challenged, large assailant made me and the tenants extremely uncomfortable – he had a proclivity to corner women – until a skydiving mentor appeared and I told him I'd wanted to shoot the assailant in the face but had instead pounded his head in with a shovel. I thought he was dead – but his mother nursed him back to consciousness.

Three days later:

Intense, enjoyable make-out session with One of the Loves of My Life [the ex who inspired my book To Whom I Could Have Been: A True Love Story*] – with some verbal. Nice.*

Subsequently: a foursome with three stylish guys in a loft that seemed to belong to Dad – he largely left us alone and behaved and stayed in the living room. I had to shit, which I did in yet another of those exposed toilets situated in the middle of a room that afford no privacy. Took so long the guys almost left; I caught them in the nick of time. Really liked relaxing into how they had to wait because I was in charge.

And then, a week after that:

A house I shared with others – although I'd thought the pool was

235

mine. Floated around after getting naked and drinking rainwater collected in a cup. Others' floatation devices strewn about; people appeared.

Adventure.

Hiked in a faraway land; then turned up at a collective living complex with common bathrooms, where various dreambeings lived.

On my way to a funeral – one or two of the dreambeings led us – and, once there, I climbed down a fire escape and swung to the ground. (Realized I'd been naked in the wrong body and felt sexually aroused / embarrassed about it.)

The dreambeings awoke some other woman, who'd been sleeping in a bathtub on a circus truck, whereupon this happy cadre of Muppets awoke with her and rose, one by one. We talked about skydiving – 150, 155 jumps – being a newbie – and she encouraged me.

Hint of Something More

As the dreamclusters unfold and collide, of course, I continue with the EMDR. Only now, whereas in the beginning I was utilizing a desktop computer screen and moving my eyes to the left and right, back and forth, across the lines of light, at this point, out of wonder, I up my game to streaming 360-degree DMT visuals – with vr goggles. Vivid colors and intricate designs spread out in all directions around me, and I can turn my head and follow the movement in this spherical psychic womb, whenever so compelled.

Yearning to trigger even more effective mind-body integration, meanwhile, I listen to music over noise-cancelling headphones – trance seems to work especially well – and twirl the Baoding balls in circles with my hands. The tingling, smooth metal ball surfaces caress areas of my palms and fingers that normally go unnoticed.

Energy flows unobstructed through my hands, lightening them until they dance in harmony with the beats pulsing in my ears.

Chiseling away the binds of perception.

Releasing gravity into ether.

Lifting the soul.

And launching consciousness into somewhere amid the Waking and the Dreaming: an In Between, somewhere the two realms meet and overlap, infusing one another with their individual characteristics, generating uniqueness and blurring any distinction that might separate them.

As this whirlwind of activity submerges my senses, I replay the prior night's dreams, which, stirred up and polished like stones on a riverbed struck by flash-flooding, erupt into view, sparkling and pristine.

I don't really know why or how these techniques work.

Only that they do.

Somehow – perhaps not each and every time, but often enough, nonetheless – the mind-body integration exercises connect me to dreamthreads that I thought I'd lost, or which I grazed for an instant upon awakening but inadvertently let go of on my way to the bathroom or when starting my coffee or whatever; and, by massaging interpretive pathways, these techniques also facilitate receipt of Messages and identification of dreambeings, especially troublemakers, tricksters and foes.

*

Two-headed person where I, the girl, wake after all this time and end up falling for the guy on my other side. He reaches his arms around me – and I do the same – for us to hug. I feel so safe and warm.

We get sliced apart, and he's like, "Oh, when this happens, it just numbs out and we meld back together." Except, this time, we ultimately tumble and blend into a single, slightly angry dreambeing that rules over a cult of followers.

Suddenly I'm separate, hovering. The followers tumble, too – like, off a cliff where everyone resides. I'm trying to take it right to the limit and impress the guy without getting too hurt or dying.

Hey, what's this lingering feeling of that tall thin tree I used to climb, when I was little…

*

Well, check *this* out. Wtf.

Here I am, a couple of years into my dreaming practice and around jump 150 – yes, you've sensed it, the Dreaming and the sky are heading toward Convergence in this story – on a run in Crystal Cove, peering down at the canyon, you know, right where I paused for a tree bath back in *Month Two: Noticing.*

EMDRing dreams, for me, tends to lend the Waking a luster that persists two or three hours afterward – as though everything I'm seeing, or, perhaps, my vision itself, has enlivened.

So too this particular morning, when, sure enough, I removed my vr goggles and headphones in awe, emerging from the belly of the very beast I've grappled with ever since depression first installed itself overhead in junior high: the brutality we endure from feeling alone, and unloved.

Fuck that shit.

All my baggage, like an old skin, has been shed.

I feel lighter.

Faintly winged.

Below, the world glistens and floats. Sunlight pierces tree cover on the gorge floor: The grove shimmers, I imagine, with spiderwebs strung from one trunk or branch to another, electrified in the morning brightness like illuminations that connect lovers.

What strikes me among so much glimmer is interconnectivity – and how this moment transcends both space and time.

For, you feel me, look: I am breathing, as you are now, air that those leaves are exhaling...

our existence depends on them and...

these same trees were producing oxygen into the same atmosphere that swirled around our planet and gathered into the wind that kept me alive atop a mountain in Petra so long ago...

wind from same air we get to fly through whenever we leave an airplane door.

*

As the theoretical physicist Carlo Rovelli observes in his book *The Order of Time*: "We can say: I see a table, a chair, a pen, the ceiling – and that between myself and the table there is nothing. Or we can say that between one and another of these things there is air. Sometimes we speak of air as if it were something, sometimes as if it were nothing. Sometimes as if it were there, sometimes as if it were not there. We are used to saying 'This glass is empty' in order to say that it is full of air. We can consequently think of the world around us as 'almost empty,' with just a few objects here and there, or alternatively as 'completely full' of air."

*

I gaze out across Orange County at the Santa Ana Mountains – on the other side of which I did my first night jump over in Lake Elsinore, beyond which, a little further, lies my "home" dz (as if they all don't feel like home), the place on this earth where I did my first tandem skydive with the Puerto Rican – and I take in how, over the course of two decades, I have at last

241

gone full circle, and am ready to go around again.

I take a deep breath.

Of that same air.

And then I run.

Down into the canyon.

Toward the grove.

*

Oftentimes, on weekends, so many people visit Crystal Cove that the parking lot fills up and closes. Those days, I jog past groups of people everywhere – atop the seaside mountain ridges, on the canyonside trails, in the gorge.

Today is a weekday, however, and no one is around.

And so I'm here at the bottom of this canyon, in the middle of nature, miles from a bathroom – you understand, you're with me here, right?

Meh.

Go for it.

I yank down my running shorts and squat and let the tinkle flow.

At which point something happens.

As I'm an inch or two from the ground, vulnerable and exposed, underwear around my ankles, maybe splattered with two or three drops of pee, there comes, from the other side of the grove – somewhere along the path that cuts down the very center of the gorge – a man's voice, carried by wind.

"I can hear you breathe," he sings.

Shudder.

Silence.

There is nothing.

Only this breeze.

This gentle breeze laced with terror.

This air.

This beautiful, necessary, life-saving, horrifying air – tearing the fabric of reality asunder as it ventures, softly, in and out of my nostrils.

"I can hear you breathe…"

Jump 208: *Touch You in the Sky*

Hey, you.

Let's catch up.

There are the first eight jumps after being naked in the sky, all at the Chicks Rock Boogie thrown by Skydive Elsinore, where I spend the weekend freeflying with women – quite the experience in a sport with something like 13% female participation.

There are many two-way freefly jumps – with whomever I can muster to massacre a sit with me.

There's a handful of freefly three-ways.

The periodic freefly LO jump, whenever I can extract one from the Swarm of Freefly Boys – the Boys themselves still keep brushing me off, or maybe it's that I'm not aggressive enough – and pin him down in a plane seat next to me.

A six-way hybrid, where three of us hold a belly circle, while the other three – members of the Swarm – sting their portions of the formation into a sit and –

OMG –

WHOOSH –

The whole group's terminal velocity accelerates, breathtakingly, as if the center of the universe has caved in.

Almost every skydive transforms some part of me in some way – but this one especially.

See, it's a celebratory 300th jump for the Beaming Girl From Oregon – and my first one with the Boys – and, so, I can't help but gleam as well, inside and out, now that I am, finally, on a motherfucking skydive with the upper classmen.

Across from me: the Anvil, sunglasses hiding his eyeballs as usual, even though it's a sunset jump in early December. And, holding onto my leg straps, on either side: the Young Turk, you remember, the inverted giant sequoia tree with the white eyelashes, and our Incredibly Sweet LO.

Oh shiiiiit.

YAAASSSSSSS.

There are the canopy relative work (CReW) jumps, you know, where I deploy right out of the airplane at altitude – *oh dear, I've mucked up that exit and now I'm spinning but I can't take any more time to get stable because if I wait to pitch this goddamn CReW-specific canopy at terminal, the force could break my neck.*

Whoa.

OMG.

Now, would you believe it, here I am, less than four minutes later, high-fiving my instructor, who has wound my canopy lines around his shins and shimmied down to my head, in the sky.

You know, if one of us screws up, we could spin into in a wrap and I'd have to cut myself out with the hook knife he gave me, as we plummet in a heap toward to the earth.

Also, this parachute I'm borrowing has holes. I mean, it's obviously still jumpable – I'm flying it, right? – but, it does have holes.

I mean, what the hell?

Keep going.

Just fly.

Oh, snap – a couple of two larger group freefly attempts – like, with four or five other jumpers.

Should I really be freeflying with this many people yet?

Three wingsuit attempts.

You know the type.

Fuck. I was so looking forward to skygasms in a wingsuit – but, alas, I've been anxiety-dreaming about these jumps two nights in a row, and now I'm totally messing up each one out of apprehension, morphing upon exit into a potato chip made from lead, crumpling through the atmosphere.

Oh dear.

Another night jump – this time in a group of three, wherein the Mexican randomly goes to a sit, for some reason, and drops away from us, down into the dark abyss, and I look over at the Israeli in freefall and we're like WTF.

And jump 199, where the Incredibly Sweet LO – the one who organized the hybrid and has made time to jump together before – takes me up and flies me in a head-down exit for several seconds, until we break apart and

oh

my

God

I

somehow

fly

back

to

him

and

he

touches

my knees

with

his hands

and then

I fly away

and back once more

and

extend my hand

and

he takes it

with his own.

Hey, remember, from *Month Eight: First Times*, how much I miss them? —

well,

here it is:

a first time:

my first freefly dock.

Ever.

It happened!

Just like that.

Meanwhile, there are lots of belly jumps in between because... well... because I'd been told to avoid solo freefly jumps once I'd learned to maintain stability, otherwise, left on my own, I'd develop bad habits, like backsliding, without knowing it.

Then some more skydives, of various sorts.

Until.

Jump 208.

Holy shitballs.

The Anvil is going to do a jump with me?!

I mean, I get the six-way we ended up on and all that... but... now... it's just us?

On a skydive – together?

A two-way, he and I?

Wild.

We mock-up the exit – standing there in an imaginary sky van, so he can show me how to leave the door and remain upright – or maybe we don't mock it up and he simply gives me some advice about flying a sit out of that particular aircraft.

Of course, he kinda doesn't have to — I've done all those sitfly exits into the giant television screen of the earth already, you recall — but, I'm so flattered he's jumping with me that I just smile and nod, letting my eyes glimmer, if they will.

"Giant television screen of the earth," he murmurs, hmmphing in approval.

Upon which we turn to board the plane.

And, as we lean down to grab our helmets, he whispers: "I'm going to touch you in the sky."

*

At altitude, whichever men are closest raise the door, and the giant television screen of the earth reveals what is — don't tell anyone — probably too much cloud cover to jump through.

But, look, the light has turned green, and we can see where the dropzone is — I'm choosing my words carefully here, you realize — and, so, presently, out goes the first group, and the next...

Our turn.

I look over my shoulder.

His eyeballs are concealed behind those eternal sunglasses he wears, and his face remains expressionless.

"Catch me if you can!" I yell, then slap down my visor and dash out.

Fuck it, who cares about body positioning – I wanna see this shit.

I crane my head backward – somehow maintaining stability without tumbling over as my body accelerates – and watch the Anvil leap out a half-second later, into this giant real-life television screen, now in 3-D, and come chasing after me.

Down and down we go.

Faster and faster.

Terminal velocity.

Ah, damn, he's not gonna get close enough.

That sucks.

It's still epic tho.

All this.

We're going so fast.

Hey wait.

Here he comes.

Inching closer.

Closer and closer.

Fuck, he's so close.

But this skydive's almost over.

So close.

So very close.

OMG.

Here it is.

His hand.

The midnight black of his skin.

Encircling the pale moon of mine.

Right before…

we go speeding through a cloud.

Healing

It's been exactly two weeks since I was touched in the sky. I started *The Art of Dreaming* by Carlos Castaneda yesterday, and, in my dreams last night, I fucking encountered a scout and found my own hands in the very first dreamsequence afterward:

In a magical swamp-city land that eventually becomes New York, getting ready for Armageddon – along with my brother J. and Mom and Dad and maybe some alternating-identity others. I do manage to notice some details from the outset – including a glowing fish skeleton that rises to the surface of a pond where I am walking on a quasi-gangplank... and then submerges into dark water below. (Holy fuck – a scout.)

We end up on a rooftop to escape the end of the world, however, buildings begin to heave without relent: There are strong earthquakes that send the cityscape tumbling over like dominoes. I head down a series of black (and, subsequently, white) iron spiral staircases populated by people in a Magritte painting, talking about law school. Happiness wells up within me over being done, or almost done, with that crap, for education – and particularly higher education, especially law school – gears toward annihilation of the individual and destruction of creativity and the self. Impatience nearly overcomes me.

Meanwhile, the buildings continue falling, and, the next thing I know, I am losing Dad and Mom and J. as I run from one overturning rooftop to the next, propelled like on a hamster wheel across edifices.

Finally, the ground. A couple of huge rats, hunkered inside crusty light brownish cocoons with goo and ingrown hairs, dangle the from low-hanging cave walls that surround me; I figure they've come to eat the dead people all around (though there aren't any corpses in the immediate vicinity and it's too early for them to decay and reek). Fuck, I have to fend off an attack from one that seems particularly rabid and brazen. It gnaws at me before I am able to fling it off.

Now in a car with a guy I don't know, who substitutes as a family member, and we kiss in sheer terror, with wide eyes — he has the most beautiful dark brown luscious skin — though I am calmer than he. I find my hands to steer us through the rubble and drive away: our car sports a black leather interior — it is a coupe, I believe — with the steering wheel on the right side.

And then I awake.

Second sleep: at the Oscars with Mom watching this very fat opera singer or something — who is wearing a gigantic puffy black coat and a massive shimmering golden shawl. She's just finishing up a mid-presentation performance — then she scurries in a swoosh offstage — only to reappear an instant later, running along the edge of the curtain and *nearly knocking over the host as she skids out onto the shiny floor, breasts now exposed, her nipples large and mauve.*

The host topples over too, and it's a disaster as they both are whisked away. Stunned audience; go to commercials. Utter shame, embarrassment or discomfort – plus an element of rancid, unmitigated curiosity – a mixture that quickly/gradually transitions to stirred carnality – dominating the theater, the universe.

Ahh, collective relief – like a group expulsion of mind pus.

Later: three pallid, waif-like aspiring child actors (one whom I think I recognize) horde me – you know, the pandering type, playing a role as if trying to impress every single person they meet, every instant. Their eyes are almost glowing – though their irises are faded but also strangely lulling. I remain wary as a matter of prudence.

At some point I catch a glimpse of Madonna strutting by in the distance – her fake ponytail billowing like a mane – and I marvel that she moves very lithely for a 60-year-old.

At another point, I am sitting next to J., who grabs a (right) testicle that suddenly manifests on my body, somewhere near my abdomen – a single, long nerve pangs and pangs and he only tightens his grip as I beg him to let go.

*

What astonishes me most: the scout was so much like the

one Castaneda wrote about in his own first encounter (read the book, it's soooooo good); and, I escaped into wakefulness the very instant I needed to by the (apparently challenging) active dreaming practice technique of finding my own hands.

Hey, wait a minute.

Did I locate my hands in my previous cutaway dreams?

I'll have to start paying closer attention.

*

The healing dreams – softening embraces between the Dreaming and the Waking, which budded around a Hint of Something More – effervesce as I progress in this journey: beyond the initial brainflush, beyond those first dreamclusters and their messy convergences, beyond the neuroses and dreck and spiritual scum and strife of conflicting forces and emotions: the stream of growing pains and almost hallucinatory fevers that seemed, at the time, to cramp and retard me, but which were, I can begin to better see, essential and necessary components of learning, of becoming stronger and getting to know features of myself – and reality – that I'd ignored way too long.

Feel me?

Reach out, through the ether, and let's touch.

You and me.

We're on a skydive together.

We're flying through the clouds.

*

A distinguishing feature of this next phase of the Dreaming that I've entered is – in contrast to the many solo, isolating adventures I'd gone on up to now – how well-peopled my nightly excursions have become.

And the dreamsex. My god.

There are some truly awesome orgies – typically with a group of men, which is always nice – as well as delightful windows of voyeurism and vicarious pleasure that pop up like flowers. It's a new dreamplace for me, this emotional paradise, where I finally just say *Fuck it* and relax into whatever body the Dreaming installs me within – male or female or a combination of both – and subversively relish one unexpected interchange after another.

Bliss.

Meanwhile, ever more emissaries and troublemakers and foes – some of which I identify immediately as inorganic beings, that is, streaks of energy from who-the-fuck knows where, and others, whose identities and origins remain unclear – make their appearances.

I may mistake what these presences are from time to time, however, increasing familiarity has eased me into a dreamversion of the social contract, replete with terms and conditions for engagement with them: contempt and even disdain, where appropriate, but also tolerance, and even, in some instances – who would've guessed – affection.

I mean, it makes sense.

We all have to get along, don't we.

*

I go through a dreamcluster of self-love and wonderment, where I attend museum exhibits and discover books about my own little life: communications from Beyond that staying alive is, in fact, worth it.

And I find myself dreamdeciding and dreamwilling and dreamfeeling and dreamthinking with greater facility and ease, not to mention improved dreamattention. For the first time in many years, as I alluded to at the beginning, back in *Month One: The Change*, I awaken more and more frequently from *real rest*.

You know.

The sleep we yearn for.

The touch of angels that restores.

The gentle suggestion there's something more.

*

Epic search dream. In a wilderness-surrounded house at the top of a hill that doubles as a base camp and a jumping off place. I'm in the process of a project — organizing / winnowing — and my valuables get stolen — though only the objects I actually care about, including my wallet. I run around trying to figure out who it was, questioning people — soon enough I even tell a guy to clear out of his room so I can cast a spell — and I try my damnedest, straining to will my stuff back to me through the Dreaming.

There is a sort of plant-related experiment clustered around some of my remaining belongings — things I don't give a damn about. Turns out one of the wingsuit organizers from my home dz has taken them — she materializes as an imposter — to conduct some sort of initiation ritual. She laughs in the darkness. I don't think it's funny, but also I'm flattered to be getting initiated.

Suddenly I'm driving adjacent to her — a Waking version of her this time, I believe — talking as if she's in the same car, until I realize she can't hear me because she isn't. I think she's turning left and so I do, as well — but, again, she isn't — and now there's a car chase and someone is coming madly toward me and I gotta swerve over the ruffage and back onto the main road.

Oh, my: this house! (It's within a clearing in a forest, hidden away like – my god, it's my own version of The Cone from Thomas Bernhard's novel Correction *– it has a personality and the details of it are alive: These motherfuckers are some manifestly living inanimate details, for sure).*

Shit, the road to up here has just gotten steeper and steeper and, from the relentless rain, more and more riddled with crevices – threatening to render it untraversable – even by evolving car or flying bike – or whatever contraption this is.

Fuck wow I'm on the roof and rappelling down into a window to go to the bathroom. (It's relatively open-plan, like some of the public restrooms I've dreamed into before, except by now I've learned to engage better and create and enjoy some privacy notwithstanding the voices outside.)

Hmm. A bit later I'm amongst a group at the house and something very strange is happening to us, as reality breaks down and we go into a sort of overwhelming trip. Cotton mouth. Everything slows down, nearly grinding to a halt; movement is molasses and control is sapped away; we melt into the universe which is pinpointed where we are; and I encounter realizations about personal power and strength, which I suddenly encounter / find / muster up despite myself and against all odds, as the fabric of the universe further dissolves and disintegrates around the edges to reveal a horror-like eternal underlay and confrontational foundation / layer of how things really are.

We are all getting Messages from another place — transmitted by inorganic beings or other essences in a demonic — but necessary, and abrasive and discomforting but nevertheless possibly not harmful — spirit or occurrence realm, Elsewhere. The Message I receive is, basically: If you just persist and stick with it, everything will be okay.

I am the first to receive a Message, but then the others' messages come, too, and things improve slightly, as our individual volition starts to return.

Later: aha, here we go: I'm in a warehouse of my stuff, getting ready to dispense with it forever — there are upscale gowns and blouses that I don't exactly recognize and don't feel anything much for — this sequence feels like when I weeded through my New York closet at Goodbye Time and tossed out virtually everything — at which point I realize I'm in the Dreaming.

I reach out to grab a bright green dress, it's the same vivid color as the bright green shirt I discarded from my New York closet in the Waking, not long ago — it shimmers with little circles-flaps, like my purple curtains at home in Los Angeles in the Waking — and I see my hands. I also catch sight of belongings on the top shelf, above me, writing pads I think — but I don't really care enough to look and find out more.

Some people are helping me — they're a bit intrusive and nosey. But, since I understand it's the Dreaming by this point, I relinquish any remaining hold and let it all go.

Oh, my stars: liberation, lightness — if a bit poignant and vaguely bittersweet. Goodbyes are hellos to whatever's next.

Black Holes

Do you remember the first image of a black hole we ever saw, spreading like wildfire across the Internet? Yeah, the deeply orange and black glowing glob that resembles a devil tiger's eye?

*

"Sign me up," I messaged the Broad-shouldered Former Marine.

I mean, why the hell not.

Sure, I hadn't been planning on it exactly.

But, sooner or later, I was gonna do it.

I mean, I'd been keeping a mental list of "things I'd never do" in skydiving – and going through each item, one by one.

1. Look: I just wanted to cross a tandem off the bucket list – I'd never jump out of an airplane unattached to a professional.

1a. Oh my God, an unattached skydive was the most extraordinary experience of my life.

2. Okay I'm 41 – all I want to do is see if I can survive 7 jumps for my AFF course. I'd never do more than that, or jump alone. No way.

2a. Oh my God, my first solo jump after completing AFF has blown my fucking mind.

3. I'll stop after getting my A-license at 25 jumps. Anything beyond that is absurd.

3a. Oh my God, I got my A-license like five jumps ago and they've already got me doing four-ways, six-ways, seven-ways… We get a 3% discount for buying blocks of tickets in cash? Fantastic.

4. I will stop after my first cutaway. For sure.

4a. I'll stop after my second cutaway.

5. I do not need to downsize from a 190.

5a. Oh my God, I thought flying a 170 was incredible but this 150 is really something.

5b. I think poor body position contributed to my second cutaway – I need to keep working on it.

6. I will never, ever do a nighttime skydive.

6a. Oh my God, skydiving at night is spiritual transformation.

7. Tunnel time? With those fees?

7a. Oh my God, 20 minutes of tunnel time was really helpful.

8. Freeflying is totally insa-

8a. WHEEEEEE!

9. But still, I probably would not do something like a 10-way

or group freefly with strangers…

9a. WHEEEEEE! WHEEEEEE!

10. More tunnel time? With those fees? Are you fucking crazy?

10a. Oh. My. God. When. Can. I. Go. Back.

*

That was the first six months. And, as you already know, the CReW and wingsuiting and all the rest came toppling like a house of cards shortly thereafter.

So, I mean – why the hell not?

Look. I'll admit it.

Two other coincidences made this decision inevitable.

The first was that I was going to be nearby, up in Ogden, Utah, already, for training from the world-renowned wind tunnel coaches there. (Travel for tunnel was another item that "I'd never do" – a little further down the list.)

Second, and, even more persuasive, there was the Carpenter connection.

You see, before I'd met him, the Carpenter had done some acting and film work in Hollywood. One of his projects involved stunts for a blockbuster, on the set of which he became acquainted with notorious BASE jumper Miles

Daisher. What's more, the Carpenter and Miles had not only done a movie together – they'd also run into each other, serendipitously, in Cabo San Lucas.

So, there it was.

Could there really be any question why the hell I wouldn't – I mean, really, any question at all – say *Yes* to my first BASE jump course, taught by Miles Daisher, at Perrine Bridge in Twin Falls?

*

I hadn't been to Utah since that random high school skiing trip a quarter of a century ago; I couldn't remember ever having been to Idaho before.

The landscape splayed out in every direction – a topographic tapestry of open plains bursting up here and there, and everywhere, into startling mountain ranges, the peaks of which kinda reminded me of the position I used to strike, arching up in bed, gasping, whenever One of the Loves of My Life kissed the back of my knees.

I drove and drove.

And drove.

Overhead, the sky tossed and turned in between cloudy and rainy and sunny and clear – likewise reminding me of being in bed with One of the Loves of My Life, when I used to get overcome with emotion I wished would never stop undulating, never stop swelling in universal revolutions, never stop hurtling me in alterations among adoration and lust.

And, whoa.

Once I reached my destination and turned onto the quiet road at the end of which nestled the house where we'd be staying, my eyes opened in rapture: A rainbow hinted through the sea of mist above the gorge we'd be flinging ourselves into tomorrow.

*

Each of us reacts uniquely.

The Little Hot Guy, lean as a marathoner and as exuberant as an elf, bounds about the living room and into the kitchen – hopping from the floor where he slept, through the walkway and to the countertop where his tea sits brewing, and then back again – all in a second, it seems. Periodically he *whoots* or hollers, or emits other noises expressing nervous excitement and glee.

Or whatever we're all feeling.

The Hot, Deliberate Move Guy – whose face could be statuary displayed in a museum, and whose upper body comprises mostly arms, such very nice deltoids extending what seems like an entire football field down to a set of perfectly formed, slow-and-intentionally-moving hands – remains largely quiet. You know, just sort of walking around finalizing things, not real things necessarily, but things nonetheless.

The Broad-shouldered Former Marine, meanwhile, gets angry, exploding over the disappearance of... whatever it is he's looking for. Everyone understands.

And I – well, I'm not sure how I'm reacting, at least not how my instincts have defaulted into confronting the dramatically increased likelihood of impending death – though I do know, here on the inside, that I'm convinced I'm going to perish.

You know.

That I'm not actually finishing my coffee – as if everything's normal.

That I'm not showering and getting dressed – like any other day.

That I'm not in the car driving back down that curving roadway I drove up last evening, and then across this weird corner of some once glorious town, a slice of small-town America chockful of fast food franchises and chain stores and gas stations, toward the Bridge.

That, as our jumping off place comes into sight, my brain is not sizzling, and thought and emotion are not setting off like Pop Rocks in my fucking head.

That I am not stepping into the leg straps of a BASE rig that someone else, somewhere, but who knows who or where, has packed with a single canopy, and no reserve.

That I am not tightening the chest strap.

Or following my group, as we head under the walkway and up the stairs around the corner.

Or making my way across the Bridge – as onlookers gawk, blanketing this netherspot of non-reality in eerie, dirty silence, their saliva almost palpable through the faraway non-distance separating them from us: we, who have become objects, seen through the onlookers' conflicting sense of awe and desire for carnage: we, these totally crazy people, these nut jobs, these thrill-seeking death flirts, these maniacs whose eyes flame wildly like nothing I've ever seen before: afire in a rim of devil tiger orange delineating otherwise all-encompassing, matter-gulping, rationality-devouring black pupils: Fuck, I *have* seen those images that our eyes have become: They look like that black hole: the horror in us.

Us.

Oh my God.

It's him.

Now him.

Now him.

Now me.

I'm climbing over the railing.

I'm standing there.

Here.

It's my turn.

My turn to jump.

To jump –

To –

My eyes.

Oh God – my eyes.

What am I seeing?

*

I would not give up the vortex – this instant of eternity opening up and simultaneously closing forever – that chasms between the second when my feet leave the Bridge and my canopy flowers overhead, a forever neverness in which my gaze shoots out toward the horizon and the world careens away and detonates toward me, with a force beyond the imagination, and the universe lights up –

I would not give it up – for anything.

It'd be worth dying for.

*

Yesterday I got to be reminded that life is about how many times we get back up again. On my second BASE jump, I had flown into a tree. I could come up with various excuses and explanations, but I think the real reason is that I was (and always will be) still learning, and mistakes we find a way to walk away from are part of this process. I need to remember that perfection remains the moon to shoot for rather than any measure of success.

Going back to the Bridge for a third jump ranks among the hardest things I have ever done. A stream of nightmare scenarios kept running through my thoughts, and, with my confidence shaken, I came up with a psychosomatic back injury and almost convinced myself that the tree landing had ruined me forever. Things escalated to utterly gnarly in my head.

But, in the end, a desire for redemption overcame everything else and so I opted to send it. Lifted by the support of my teammates and mentoring from Miles, I climbed over the railing and jumped again.

Right after I pitched – in that eternity of an instant before canopy deployment – I heard Miles exclaim, "Nice!" And then, the next thing

I knew, I was reaching for my toggles and steering where I'd planned to go.

I met the ground with a Tinkerbell landing somehow — and the joy that surged through me only kept coming as I watched the video later and heard Miles and my teammates cheer.

*

I didn't mention in that social media post how, after the second jump, I'd called the Carpenter and sat there talking to him in the parking lot at the Bridge, waiting for my group to climb back up, over the gorge wall.

Sensibly, he agreed that I'd done the right thing, sitting the next one out.

And that I needn't do another, either this evening or tomorrow or ever again, because two BASE jumps were more than I'd ever needed to begin with, let's get real, one was more than enough.

More than enough.

More.

*

At which point Miles appears next to my car window, and he and the Carpenter shoot the shit.

They haven't spoken since Cabo, or the movie, whichever

came last.

And now here they are.

In the vortex.

That's probably when I know, deep down inside.

You're with me: when I sense, without even needing to know: that, as soon as I muster whatever got me off the Bridge in the first place, I'll go again.

Again.

More.

Please.

One more time.

The Intersection: Oblivion

More bodyflight training — in a dreamplace — and it has to be done strategically, carefully, in order for me to take it to another realm of consciousness, which I so very much want to vault into and explore. In a group and must be intentional about those dynamics, as well. One of my feet may be intermittently replaced with a prothesis. The stakes are high because the next level is oblivion — though this goal may be swallowed into the heat and lava — a new state beyond the Threshold (which is neither better nor worse than ones before — it just IS).

Meanwhile, at one point, I walk into a room to get introduced to a freefly team so I can do video for them and I note one of the members' behavioral inconsistencies as to the others — but I tell myself not to judge based solely on appearances. That alluring darkness...

*

Nostalgia dream for the New York apartment, in which I'm walking around the East Village and then stopping outside the building (not my old building, but now, instead, an old house / mansion), with someone, on a possibly court-related mission that also has to do with the health of a dog I used to have / not have, and then

I WAKE UP FROM THE DREAM

INTO A DREAM

WHERE I'M IN BED WAKING UP
IN LOS ANGELES.

But I don't actually wake up yet, at least not into the Waking, and I'm grateful for everything I have, i.e., the skydiving, and I think, in particular, about the tunnel and some (nonexistent) jumping event. Then I'm with the Puerto Rican from my very first skydive and we're in bed together and he lies down and I cuddle up next to him and kiss him, but only a little (because I'm worried about my breath, of course) – and then there's something about his canopy, which I'm suddenly pulling over us for an inspection. Also worried about bugs – picking them off with my teeth – there's some strange insect that moves around on the human body, like a tiny piece of grass or otherwise deceptive bit of plant nature, and it's hard to remove.

Throughout these dreamsequences, I dreamrealize, I've been grappling with resolving irreconcilabilities among my consciousness and the Dreaming and the Waking. An inorganic being materialized in the bedroom when I was with the Puerto Rican, for example; however, I disregarded her troublemaking interference so I could commune with him.

You know, peacefully.

In oblivion.

The realm at the tips of each skydive, each dream.

Each plane ride I leap out the door, each night I drift off to sleep – lulled and yet tantalized in the sky and my bed: I let go into the emboldening humility that comes from yielding to, while simultaneously engaging with, powerlessness over forces beyond human control.

Anything can happen.

Here, in this intersection.

Where extremes meet.

The heart

of

oblivion.

The Portal: Reminiscences

The Netflix miniseries *Russian Doll* was shot in my old neighborhood in New York. I went by all those film locations thousands of times – Alan's character lives half a block from the apartment I moved out of (two weeks before I watched the show) – and I used to buy avocados from the bodega where Nadia's mom (Chloe Sevigny) got the watermelons.

Back in the 1990s, one time I was talking with Chloe in her dressing room (at a play I helped produce while working for the theater company I mentioned in *Month Four: Nipples, Dicks and the Start*) and I kissed her naked shoulder. We hung out and stuff periodically… another time I arranged for us to privately view some wood carvings at the Met on a morning it was closed to the public… an organist was practicing and music filled the otherwise empty museum… as if we were in a movie…

Anyway, she and I drifted out of touch until we ran into each other two decades later at the Russian & Turkish Baths, which is a few blocks from the bodega. When I told her who I used to be, she goes, "Holy shit, I didn't even recognize you!"

And there's more.

Nadia's character (Natasha Lyonne) lives on 5th Street and

Avenue B, which is half a block from where I lived right before that last apartment of mine near Alan's. Would you believe I saw Natasha on Avenue B several years ago – not long after she starred in a play produced by the same theater company I worked for back when we produced the play Chloe was in. Yeah so Natasha and I were crossing the street in opposite directions at Tompkins Square Park – catty-corner to the bar where her character always walks by, and where she and Alan go to get drunk.

It's like, I mean, *really*.

*

TFW you've been flying shoddily all afternoon because your back layouts and carving suck and then suddenly you realize, *hey, there's another dude in here* and so you're like *why the hell not* and you relax into your first tunnel 3-way, and, what do you know, there's your first group freefly tunnel dock – and then, later, on the way home, atop this cloud where you remain, you find yourself reminiscing over an ex – yeah, the guy you fell for on that trip down to Mexico a decade ago, One of the Loves of Your Life – when all of a sudden he calls and you're like, "Hey, I was just thinking about you," and he asks what was running through your mind and you're like, "I just love how we still get to see each other once or twice a year and have sex and it's about that time, isn't it," whereupon he goes, "Look to your right," and so you do and there he is, in the adjacent lane, smiling and waving, and you both laugh as you continue speeding down the 10 toward those gorgeous oranges and lavenders of a Los Angeles sunset – you guys catch up for a sec and then he goes, "I can't believe I'm just driving next to you on the freeway, I wasn't even supposed to be over here, I took a wrong turn," and you're like, "Oh, man – that's nothing, seriously – have you seen *Russian Doll* yet?"

*

The tunnel is, I think, some sort of Portal to an Elsewhere...

A week later, right around the same spot on the 10, I happened to be reminiscing about my First Love (she'd posted something earlier and suddenly those 25-year-old memories flooded me), when, wouldn't you know it, our song – *Closer to Fine* by the Indigo Girls – came on the radio...

It was, of course, followed shortly thereafter by *The Lovecats*, which is, in turn, one of the many songs by The Cure that remind me of another First – the First Girl I Ever Kissed... oh my God, holy shit, now *that* motherfucking memory has almost turned 30, Jesus, how relentless...

Anyway, when *Lovecats* concluded, I switched stations, curious what would happen next...

And so it was that I landed immediately on a cover of another Cure masterpiece, *Lovesong*, which just tickled all the more because it's yet another from the soundtrack of our relationship, the First Girl I Ever Kissed and mine...

I guess I write about these experiences to remember that they really happened, that the underlying memories must be just as real as well, and that reality itself infuses each day with a dream that keeps ebbing and flowing into oceans of time and wow...

Thus life remains neither what I imagined nor would have asked for – I always hoped that one of these Loves might last ever so much closer to forever and we'd share a lifetime of memories together, rather than this lifetime of memories I have ended up sharing with Countless Loves – but, hey, things could be a whole lot worse and perhaps now I can simply do what I'm slowly learning in the tunnel, the Portal: relax into the speed at which it's all flying by and let myself lift...

into air...

Jumps 264, 299 and 300: *Closer*

14. Angle jumps?! Too dangerous.

14a. Wow – this angle camp has changed my life. The Skydiving Beast strikes again: I got lucky on our 2nd and 3rd jumps, but, tbh, I have been chasing the group on every other skydive this entire weekend. It's awful. My logbook includes entries such as: "I suck." "I still suck." "Miserable." I am so disappointed in myself that I get into the car and leave before one last jump. *I'm going to give up skydiving*, I decide. *I'm useless.* But, then, at the first stoplight I hit on the four-hour drive to Vegas, where I'm going to stay the night before heading up to Ogden – wait, why am I going there for tunnel training, if I'm going to stop jumping? – I find myself declaring, out loud, "I am not a quitter!" So, I swing a U-turn, speed back to the dz, hop on the plane and – FINALLY – end up in proximity with the group for a few seconds.

Jump 264 is in the books.

*

The LO with the angular jawlines.

Yeah, the first LO I ever tried freeflying with.

Here we are again.

Jump 299.

A head-down skydive together – the first one where I can feel myself...

giving in...

relaxing...

and smiling back.

*

Hey, look – here we are, together once more, on jump 300 – an angle, our second skydive in a row today – and, will you fucking look at that, here you are, right above me, tracking across the sky, so near my eyes I see the stubble heavily dusted across those angular jawlines of yours.

"You were close enough for me to kick your chest," you say, once we're back on the ground.

Is that a thing – kicking people in the chest on an angle jump?

"Yeah," I ruminate, "that's the closest angle I've ever been on."

*

Funny how we have to work so hard, exert so much time and energy, spend so many dollars and hours and minutes –

hurling years of life-force into oblivion – all to learn one thing:

How to relax.

And let go.

And fly.

Within a Dream

Dreamwake to a dream within a dream. Nested dream: a dreamsequence that meanders into a sort of auditorium, where I join some other women in box seats up above — feels very high school-y, like maybe a teacher has organized the event or something. We are here to observe the beginning of a play and get things started somehow.

I am surprised to see that we are leaving almost right after the beginning — I thought one of the women would want to stay. (Are they go-with-it emissaries?)

At some point, I'm skinny dipping in a pool with a freefly LO from the Waking and maybe a few other skydivers. Some girl comes up to me in the water and offers to lend me her bikini bottom because it's too small for her (but, I dreamthink, I went through surgery and everything, why would I do that?).

Either before or after, we are in one of the women's apartment, or possibly her house, hunching over a laptop and watching video footage. I'm like who is that person-shape of dancing sparkles — there are glass beads like painted onto a woman's figure from behind — her body moves as reflective liquid, a robot creation or something out of a movie — but then the image turns around and I see the front and it's I — I am the shimmering being.

I sheepishly ask if we can play the footage again — but the woman is onto me and she's not going to have any of it and I feel ego-centrical and small and found out.

And, so, to escape, I wake up... to another dream within this one... in which I dreamthink, "That was so vivid I have to go write it down, but I'm tired so I'll wait..." — just like I do normally except that I'm not awake into the Waking yet... but then I do wake shortly thereafter.

Wait, hold on... I've woken into a skydiving dream, in which I am going too fast through the air — I cannot slow down — I am rushing and rushing toward a gigantic formation below — they are a belly group and somehow I am heading straight for them — I have to pull very high and then immediately grab my rears to steer — this action causes the inflation of my canopy to stall — oh fuck I am rushing out of the sky with a partially inflated main — it won't open — it won't open — it won't open — so at last I cutaway... and awake.

*

Two days before, I'd been on a head-down jump with the Young Turk.

"Wanna do a two-way?" he had asked.

"Sure," I had said, after a pause, trying to play it cool. "Why not?"

He manifested us, and, a few minutes later, we stood face-to-face, in the door to the mock-up, going through our exit, holding hands – as we would be doing again shortly thereafter, 12,500 feet above the earth.

*

Once that dream of a jump had passed, I ran into the Anvil in the parking lot. He goaded me to amp up my landing game, and showed me – by swerving that triangular back of his across two parking spaces, as if he were a giant flying saucer – how to swoop.

Oh shit.

Check it out.

He wants me to excel and become a sick ninja – just like he and the other Boys.

*

Boys.

On the drive back home, my thoughts drift from these two to another: the Carpenter.

I consider how exquisitely those beautiful hands of his have held our friendship these past few years – just as gently, come to think of it, as the Young Turk took my hand in the door of the airplane on our jump together, and likewise as the Anvil gestured and demonstrated canopy angles during our conversation, with his.

Yeah so here's the deal.

Everything since I almost killed myself happened only because I didn't, and, sad though it makes me to remember unrequited love, I remain grateful that the Carpenter reciprocated with friendship, instead of an affair.

For, if we had started down a different road together, then none of what you've read would have happened.

I would not have paused each morning to notice at least one thing worth living for from the day before.

I would never have learned to fly.

The Dreaming would have remained unknown to me.

And I wouldn't have met those two skybrothers – or any of the others.

So.

You see what I'm getting at.

This – all this – is why we call it falling in love, and not standing.

You know.

I know you do.

When we look into each other's eyes.

As we freefall together.

Freefall into love.

You know.

We're the same.

You and the Shimmering I.

Looking into each other's eyes.

Venturing a little closer to forever.

Expanding until our spheres of awareness overlap.

And we reach out and touch.

This instant of eternity together.

Epilogue

I took three trips to Utah that spring – four, if you count the BASE interlude bisecting the first sojourn – for tunnel training with the coaches in Ogden.

Each time, on the drive up there, I saw a car accident on the 15, about half-way between Las Vegas and Salt Lake City. In number one, it appeared that a semi and two or three cars had skidded off the highway. Number two was when the sky clouded over and started hailing – quite suddenly, before anyone could slow down – and the car in front of me fishtailed, and then swerved off the shoulder, into a ditch. Number three, yet another off-road mess, involved a couple of cars that collided near a lake outside Cedar City – right around where I happened to have not only one, but two conversations with a college friend of mine, about how to find meaning in life now that we're older.

I could not help but appreciate the import of these accidents, which served, for me, as reminders of how vulnerable I am, especially when I lapse into complacency.

It's more than just falling asleep – a very odd evolutionary feature, if you stop and think about it, entering a state of total defenselessness on a nightly basis. It's more than just leaping from an airplane – a very odd activity, if you stop and think about it, intentionally entering an emergency.

Because of whatever compulsion drives us to seek splendor.

Anyway.

You know the feeling I am getting at?

The one that descends, like a hurricane, after a close scrape or horrible loss?

The searing gratitude that the breath we just drew was not our last?

I know you do.

*

It is shortly after the third accident on the 15, as I emerge from a wave of survivor's guilt, and switch around satellite radio stations, trying to find something good, that I chance upon a broadcast of the BottleRock Festival, live from Napa, California, and crank up the volume: I love Imagine Dragons.

And by love, I mean, like, whoa.

What a surprise to hear Dan Reynolds speak so openly, in between songs, about his struggle with depression, which, he relates rawly, began in junior high.

Wow – check this shit out: He's opening up about how he started seeing a therapist back then, as a kid, and has continued with therapy ever since.

Good heavens, now he's talking about how we, as a society, must end the stigmatization of depression.

And how, even if we are depressed or in need of help, we're not broken. We're still us.

It's raining heavily now – not quite as intensely as the hailstorm moments ago – but in a torrential waterfall from the sky, nonetheless.

He's pleading…

I have to slow down, the rain's pouring so hard.

Pleading…

Don't crash your fucking car, Zoe – remember what you just saw.

To anyone who's ever experienced depression.

This is intense. I really can't see.

"Please," he says, out into nowhere, everywhere, for anyone listening: "never take your life from us."

*

Vegas.

I stopped there for at least a meal on each leg of each trip to Utah, and a few times I stayed overnight, to catch a Cirque du

Soleil show or just walk around.

As you've probably guessed by now: Yes, I adore Vegas.

Absolutely adore it.

I mean, where else – except perhaps in the sky or a dream – can we feel so free?

Should I go ahead at this point and relate that the BottleRock broadcast is when I learned Imagine Dragons are from… Vegas?

WTF.

*

Look, I could go on and on about the breathtaking majesty of national parks I made detours to on the Utah journeys…

I feel like we could talk forever and a day about the hike in Zion to Angels Landing, early in the morning, a mountaintop of mountaintops where, after making my way across those high, exposed rock faces – from which people have fallen and died – it seemed so right to sit down and look out at the edge of reality, tearing up with gratitude for every breath I had ever taken up to then and ever would take. ("Take" is a funny word for a breath, don't you agree, as if we are stealing?)

We could try, in vain, to put Arches into words, smiling at the paucity of language, which would fall so woefully short of the magnificent otherworldliness imbuing that place, destined to slip further and further away from our grasp, with every insignificant syllable...

But, I think, the most appropriate spot to commence closing would be Mesa Arch in Canyonlands, you know, a spot on someplace called an "Island in the Sky" – one thousand feet above massive gorges carved out of earth by the Colorado and Green Rivers.

For, as we find one another at long last, it is here where I am sitting, quietly thinking back on everything I've ever seen or done, you feel me, the sheer captivating magnitude of what it means to be alive – when, in an instant of eternity, this moment we share, a gust comes blasting up the canyon walls, and crests, enveloping us in a warm caress.

As if the air itself is a million hands of God, raising our chins softly and lifting our gaze out at a dreamscape vaster than anything we might have otherwise conceived.

Much like those faraway chasms in Petra – widened into an instant of eternity by the decades in between us – wouldn't you agree?

*

Jump 313. Just some random number, nothing special.

But still. I'm nervous because it's a new dropzone, the ground winds have just picked up for the afternoon and the fuckers are, conveniently, blowing straight across the landing area toward some power lines – oh dear – and also because, well, I'm about to leave a motherfucking airplane at altitude, and, if I weren't slightly apprehensive, then, frankly, there would be a problem.

But, look, if there's an option to jump above Moab, overlooking Arches and Canyonlands and something called an "Island in the Sky," let's get real, how can you *not* make a skydive?

At least one.

Even so.

Squished in the back of this tiny plane, where the air's getting chillier and chillier with every foot we ascend, I wonder: What in the actual fuck?

I mean, srsly.

What the hell?

Do I really need to be doing this?

Okay, red light.

Door's open.

Damn, the air *is* cold up here.

Way colder than you'd think down on that hot ass ground.

You know, the ground? Where most people stay?

Yellow light.

I gently tighten my hands around the exit grab bar, and look down.

Alright this spot's kinda long. Like srsly long.

Should I give it a sec or two – or three?

You know, like, wait unt-

Green light.

Jump.

"Always try to keep a patch of sky above your life."

– Marcel Proust, *Swann's Way*

Acknowledgments

Thank you so much to the first readers of this book: Kathy Handley, Andy Shutz, Aria Vela, Monica Belvel Wegner, and my mom, Carol Dolan.

Thank you – with all my heart – to my skyfamily, and everyone who has graciously given me life along this journey so far.

And, as always, thank you for reading.

54926898R00188

Made in the USA
San Bernardino,
CA